THE PRINCIPLES FOR TRAINING THE MIND

THE PRINCIPLES for TRAINING THE MIND

VENERABLE CHWASAN

The Principles for Training the Mind

Copyright © 2022 by Venerable Chwasan
All rights reserved.
No part of this book may be reproduced in any form without written permission from the publisher.

Published by Won Dharma Publications
361 NY-23, Claverack, NY 12513, USA
Phone 518-851-2581

Library of Congress Control Number: 2022917634

ISBN: 979-8-9869466-2-7

Cover design by Ryan Tiano and Sunghwan Yu

Printed in the Republic of Korea

CONTENTS

Translator's Foreword ... ix
Introduction ... xiii

Part I. Principles of the Mind

Chapter 1. Introduction to the Mind ... 3

The Principles of The Mind ... 5
The Reality Of The Neglected Mind ... 7
The Workings of the Mind ... 10
Mind Practice ... 14

Chapter 2. Aspects of the Mind ... 19

The Mind's Ordinary Aspect ... 22
The Mind's Linear Aspect ... 26
The Mind's Planar Aspect ... 28
The Mind's Multidimensional Aspect ... 29
The Content Of The Mind ... 31
The Mind Is Like A Tree ... 33

Chapter 3. The Mind's Content and Scope ... 37

Truth, Our True Nature, Consciousness, Feeling, And Intention ... 39
Spirit, Energy, Matter, And The Mind ... 54
Principles Of The Soul And Body ... 59
The Mind And The Workings Of Cause And Effect ... 74
The Mind, Karma, And Samsara ... 79

The Mind: Paths Of Progression And Regression	83
The Mind, Self-Cultivation, And Developing World Peace	86
The Mind And Health	89
Defilements And Great Enlightenment	93

Part II. Principles of Spiritual Cultivation

Chapter 4. What Kind of Object is the Mind?   101

Something to Be Sought	104
Something to Be Guarded	108
Something to Be Illuminated	110
Something to Be Straightened	113
Something to Be Tamed	116
Something to Be Cultivated	119
Something to Be Filled	122
Something to Be Harnessed	124
Something to Be Purified	129
Something to Be Emptied	133

Chapter 5. Practice to Cultivate the Mind   139

Spiritual Practice	141
Reason And Practice	144
The Possibilities Of Mind Practice	149
The Mind And Sensory Conditions	152
The Resources for Mind Practice	156
The Scriptures And Dharma Instructions	160
Threefold Practice: The Three Elements of The Mind's Life	164
Nine Paths for Daily Spiritual Cultivation	171
Reflections for Everyday Practice	174
How to Attain the Three Great Powers of the Mind	214
Overcoming Difficult Hurdles	218

Part III. The Reality of Spiritual Cultivation

Chapter 6. Our Spiritual Cultivation Plan — 229
- Lifetime Plan — 232
- Yearly Plan — 235
- Daily Plan — 239

Chapter 7. Our Vow and Repentance — 243

Chapter 8. Mindfulness and One Pointed Mind — 247

Chapter 9. Obstacles to Spiritual Cultivation — 257

Chapter 10. Diary for Spiritual Practice — 265
- The Dharma of Keeping A Daily Mindfulness Journal — 271
- The Dharma of Keeping A Mind Diary — 276

Chapter 11. The Stages of Mind Practice — 281
- The Four Stages of the Mind — 288
- Six Stages of Dharma — 290
- The Six Stages of Practice — 292
- The Pinnacle of Practice — 294

A Final Word — 303
About the Author — 305

Translator's Foreword

The following is a story I was told by my teacher.

In a small American town, there was a young man who did not get along with his father. His father was a devout Christian who insisted that his son uphold Christian values.

For his twentieth birthday, the young man begged his father to buy him a car. With great anticipation, the young man waited and wondered what type of car his father would buy him.

On the morning of his birthday, his father presented him with a tiny box. The young man assumed without question that the box would contain keys to a new car. When he opened the box, however, all he found was a single bible. He flung the bible to the ground in a fit of rage and stormed out, never to return.

Several years later, his brother called to let him know that their father had passed away and he needed to return home for the funeral. The young man hung up the phone, feeling immense regret for the many years he had gone without speaking to his father.

When he returned to his father's house, he saw many of his father's belongings scattered about the living room. On one table, he spotted the bible that his father had given him for his twentieth birthday. He opened the bible to find a letter and check inside. In the letter, his father wrote that he loved him and apologized that he could not give him more money, but hoped the check would be enough for him to purchase a car of his choice. The young man burst into tears. He regretted his acts deeply and realized that he had thrown away the car he wanted, and also the father he loved.

Likewise, many people in this world are unaware that they own something of immeasurable worth that is far more valuable than a check or any material possession. It is their Mind.

When we truly discover and use our mind, we are able to do things well and fulfill our goals. The Buddha said that everything is created by our mind. This world, along with our life, is the creation of our mind.

Sotaesan, the founding master of Won-Buddhism, said, "The study of any science has limits to its use, but if you learn how to make the mind function, this study can be utilized without a moment's interruption. Therefore, mind practice becomes the basis for all other studies." "If the mind is wholesome, everything wholesome arises along with it; if the mind is unwholesome, everything unwholesome arises along with it. Thus, the mind becomes the basis for everything wholesome and unwholesome."

Our destiny is determined by how we use our mind. When we use our mind well, our lives change for the better. For instance, if we change our pattern of being unreliable or impatient and instead become more conscientious and trustworthy, or more patient and hopeful, our life and destiny will transform.

It is truly regrettable that many people in this world do not recognize the significance of taking care of their mind. When the cart does not move forward, we are well aware that we must urge the horse, not the cart. Yet the majority of people continuously work to change their external circumstances in an effort to realize happiness in their life. This is akin to urging the cart, not the horse. The truth is that when we take good care of our mind, our lives will naturally change.

This book is all about the Mind. Spiritual practice is none other than taking care of our mind. We use this practice to train our mind to be focused, peaceful, wise, and courageous.

Jesus said, "Heaven is like a treasure buried in a piece of land. When one finds the treasure, he leaves it hidden, happily comes back home, sells everything that he owns and purchases the land. Heaven is also like a precious pearl. A merchant who is looking for such a pearl would sell everything he has to be able to buy that pearl." (Matthew, 13: 44-46)

Realizing and using our mind well is comparable to uncovering buried treasure and a precious pearl in the ocean.

This book describes in great detail a concrete and practical way to train and use our mind. These methods and principles are a light that can brighten our path to freedom and happiness.

I genuinely hope and pray that the readers' life and destiny will change as a result of reading this book.

I received assistance from numerous individuals to complete the English translation of this work. First, I would like to express my appreciation to the original translator whose work was published by

Seoul Selection Publishing House under the title *The Principle and Training of the Mind*. Based on this effort, I revised and retranslated numerous sections to make the material more accessible to all audiences and even novice practitioners. I am also indebted to numerous Won Dharma Center members. This book would not have been completed without their earnest and devoted effort in editing and refining the chapters. They will receive all the merits as a result of their sincerity and commitment.

May all sentient beings realize their original mind!
May all sentient beings be free from suffering!

Rev. Dosung Yoo
Won Dharma Center, 2022

Introduction

The mind creates our entire lives and shapes human history. It delineates the fortunes and misfortunes of individuals, including their state of calamity or happiness. And it forms our understanding of the world, its rise and fall, or its prosperity and decline.

Human civilization is the manifestation of our mind. Even materialistic and scientific perspectives that reject the true nature of the mind are the product of the mind itself. In the same way that there is a natural creator behind the phenomena of nature, there is the mind that has produced all the phenomena of human civilization.

As human beings, we are generally deficient in understanding the mind and our endeavors to inquire into it. Our practical study of the mind is sadly lacking, yet there is abundant scientific research dedicated to various objective ideas in this world. In addition, many specialized fields of study have been created to understand the mind. However, our society's understanding of the mind remains limited. Moreover, with the growth of a materialistic society, the necessity to study the mind has become increasingly urgent.

Psychology and epistemology are the academic disciplines that primarily examine the mind. In addition to studying the Way in the East, they concentrate on three core topics: existence, knowledge, and values. These fields sometimes oppose the tendencies of the material world. This book is in response to "Commentary on the Mind," which was written to address an acute and urgent need for knowledge about the mind and understanding and managing the mind. May this book shed some light on a world that has become increasingly bruised and battered by materialism.

Mind practice is immensely useful and we can witness its benefits and impact on the most significant connections in our lives, such as educational institutions, work, and families. If a more concrete approach to mind practice can be developed and widely adopted, it will be cause for celebration for ourselves and our world.

This book consists of three sections.

Part One articulates the principles of the mind. Then, an introduction to the mind is given which describes its aspects, contents, and scope.

Part Two offers a description of the principles of spiritual cultivation. First, it poses the question: what kind of object is the mind? Then it provides methods to discipline the mind through spiritual cultivation practices.

Part Three focuses on practical matters in our spiritual cultivation. Specifically, it deals with how to plan our cultivation practices, make a vow, maintain mindfulness and one-pointedness, and recognize the obstacles that hinder our cultivation.

I sincerely hope and pray that this book will help all people understand the true nature of their minds so they can ultimately attain complete liberation and make this world a better place for all humanity.

Part I
Principles of the Mind

CHAPTER 1

An Introduction to the Mind

The Principles of The Mind

Nothing in the world is self-sustaining. All things are interdependently connected. Directly or indirectly, all things can only exist through relationships of interdependence.

We rely on innumerable resources for survival, but our mind is the most fundamental and central resource of them all.

We cannot live outside the mind for even a moment. Nothing can be accomplished in the world without the use of the mind.

We generally use the term "knowledge" or "wisdom" to refer to an understanding of ethical ideas or societal principles. However, an innate, more fundamental wisdom comes from the comprehension of the principles of the mind. Unfortunately, due to our limited grasp of what we encounter daily, our attempts frequently fail. Even so, we can frequently solve problems, although a lack of knowledge is sometimes apparent.

Such unexpected outcomes highlight the importance of understanding the principles of the mind. Our acts become misguided when unwholesome desires obscure our wisdom. As a result, we inevitably choose and act in ways that lead to failure. Individuals who grasp the principles of the mind are better able to choose wisely and act on only those principles which will lead to success. As a result, they can solve problems simply and positively. Understanding the principles of the mind determines one's success and failure more than any other factor.

It is easy to neglect our mind study and practice when we get caught up in the bustling activities of our daily lives. When this happens, our uncultivated mind field becomes overgrown with all sorts of noxious plants and weeds, causing great harm to ourselves and others. The mind, however, changes into a field of gold when it is properly cultivated, producing all the fruits of grace and a bountiful harvest of happiness and freedom for ourselves and others. Which will you choose: an uncultivated field or a field of gold? This should be a matter of great concern in your life.

Cultivation of our mind is the great task that leads to eternal life. Therefore, it is an essential matter, a task of immense importance, a matter of life and death.

My hope is that this book attains my wish for all living creatures to abandon suffering and gain happiness. Let this book illuminate every aspect of the mind and help the readers to understand the mind's true nature and serve as a guide for its management and development.

The Reality of the Neglected Mind

Faith and practice represent the most mature aspect of our lives. Through them, we can enter the spiritual world. We will never transcend our simple animal nature unless we reach this higher-level spiritual world. What do we use to develop our faith and practice? Our mind, ultimately. We cannot engage in faith and practice outside of the mind. Our essential existence as human beings depends on the mind, so we must understand the mind correctly and know it completely.

In general, Koreans understand the word *maum*; however, there is said to be no equivalent word in the West. There are words with similar meanings—"mind," "heart," "soul," "spirit"—but none precisely capture the same meaning that Koreans associate with the word *maum*. Therefore, it is difficult to translate accurately.

In our pretense of knowledge, do we understand the true nature of what *maum* (heart-mind) represents? Any attempt to define *maum* will leave one short of a complete understanding. It is more accurate to say that we do not know about *maum*. There is a Korean song with the lyrics, "Your heart [*maum*], which even now I cannot fathom." Is it true that we fail to understand another's heart while knowing our own, or do we not know either? In truth, we do not completely understand our own. How often does this lead us to misuse our heart (*maum*), resulting in disaster?

Nevertheless, we have a propensity not to look deeply at our minds. As a result, the mind has become an object of apathy and neglect in modern society and an object of abuse and ridicule at times.

Understanding the true nature of our mind is not fully appreciated by our society. Despite our attempts to endure the difficulties the mind faces, we often fail to overcome such challenging situations and so give up. This happens without discrimination to all human beings from all walks of life across the globe.

We cannot help being concerned by the widespread neglect of the mind and the subsequent negative impact on contemporary society. We witness the mind losing ground to the forces of gratification, often becoming its servant. As a result, people experience much suffering.

In this state of mind, we become mere subjects of appetite, lust, excessive material wants, desire for status, thirst for power, and the pursuit for luxury and comfort. These tyrannies assail every corner of the global village.

As a result, the world of constructive ideas, powerful thinking, and contemplation, which our minds should be agents in cultivating, becomes a polluted and fallow field. The world of ethics and morality also becomes contaminated and uncultivated. The same unfortunate fate befalls the realm of belief.

Despite the severity of the daily and persistent adversities our mind faces, we take few steps to heal them. We put those issues out of our mind. We tend to fixate and overreact to the external world, yet most of us do not take an interest in addressing the unhealthy state of our mind. Because most of us are not "fixing" our minds, we pile up a veritable mountain of problems, many of which remain deep within our mind. This is the reality.

Ask yourself, is there no effect on our life when we neglect our mind? Can we continue to neglect our mind in this way?

The Workings of the Mind

Before we answer this question, let us first look at the workings of the mind. Can we succeed as human beings if the mind is unconscious? In retrospect, none of humanity's numerous astounding advancements would have been possible without the use of the mind. If our thoughts can progress us this far, then everything except natural phenomena is manufactured, and everything manufactured was created through the agency of the mind.

Our political systems with their turbulent history, our social structures, educational systems, welfare systems, culture, philosophy and thought, systems of faith and practice, and scientific discoveries are all products of the mind.

The philosophical concerns of the ancients originated long ago out of a tendency to seek out the destiny of human beings—the fortunes, misfortunes, calamity, and happiness of human life—within the mysterious workings of natural phenomena. There was a tendency to search for destiny in the stars, feng shui, natural phenomena like holy trees and great rocks, or in animals. In recent years, there have been many similar cases in which people attempted divination with squid and turtles. As science progressed, it was demonstrated that various divination were only natural phenomena, and these practices were ruled invalid. It was a culture of untruth festered by human ignorance from the imagination of groundless assumptions.

Once we understand that the mind is the driving force behind our fortunes and misfortunes, we recognize that natural phenomena do not dictate our circumstances.

What do humans truly need? We have the habit of constantly creating, no matter the cost. Our mind is an agent that perpetually establishes a history of rising and falling, prosperity and decline. It is also the agent of resolution for many circumstances that have unfolded throughout history—at all places and at all times. We have seen the unfolding of tragedy and triumph in history. Indeed, such history is being created right now. We continue to create, never resting for a moment. Here, again, the agent is the mind.

The mind creates all our destinies—our fortunes and misfortunes, calamity and happiness. Some people seek such destinies outside the mind, but this is futile. In all cases, the original executor is us, or more precisely, our mind.

The mind is the force behind this extraordinary world of cause and effect.

This is not to deny that our environment affects us, but we must acknowledge that the seed within the mind came first. The great mountains of success we build on earth and the failures that ensue when they crumble away are, in the end, the product of our mind.

Our mind contains many hidden potentials, gifts, and abilities, like seeds lying unseen beneath the earth. Like our mind, these seeds often remain dormant, unseen in the ground until they encounter an environment where all conditions are met, and only then do they sprout and grow. Then, finally, they mature and bear fruit, creating outcomes of fortune and misfortune, calamity and happiness, rising and falling, prosperity and decline, success and failure. They determine our pleasure and anger, sorrow and joy, suffering and happiness, prosperity and poverty, happiness and misfortune.

Again, the source of this cause and effect is the mind.

The extraordinary world of the karmic principle is also unfolding within our mind.

We may see extraordinary phenomena in which virtuous results come from virtuous causes and evil results from evil causes. Even then, the mind is the actor. Those who subscribe to fatalism—the four pillars, physiognomy, palmistry, divination, and the like—attempt to learn about people's future destinies in such ways. But even Ma Yi's Appearance Method, a physiognomy classic, warns us that the four pillars are not the same as physiognomy, nor is physiognomy the same as the mind image.

The mind ultimately determines all things. Without the presence of the mind, none of what we refer to as "human work" can be accomplished. Indeed, even the domain and resources of nature may be used in various ways depending on our mind-wisdom as human beings. We can produce all sorts of new creations using them as our building blocks. Whether we create ultimate bliss or hell in this world, both are the result of our mind.

Since early on, Western philosophical thought subscribed to the concept of idealism, while Buddhism followed the idea that "all things are created by the mind."

In this way, he who has come to understand the truth of what the mind does and all it can do may be said to have attained enlightenment. We must abandon the mistaken belief that we know the mind and develop a true understanding of it. We have to understand the true nature of the mind, its efficacy, its substance, and its functioning. We must understand its connection with non-arising and non-ceasing, its relationship with cause and effect; its association with rising and falling; its connection with prosperity and decay. We have to understand its connection with fortune and misfortune, as well as with calamity and happiness, prosperity and decline, birth, old age, illness, and ultimately death.

Although this is the principle, the reality is we merely emphasize and worry about the various incidents that occur, the destruction of our environment, and wrongful deeds. We show little sign of reflecting inward to address the poor state of our mind, which is the primal cause.

How can we expect to straighten out the world's affairs if we cannot first sort out our mind?

Mind Practice

We must not neglect the mind, as it is the fountain from where all these limitless possibilities flow.

Every one of our possessions must be learned in its entirety, from its structure to its functions and operation, if we intend to use it well. Similarly, we must understand our mind, know it deeply, guard it, discipline it, and study how to use it aptly and wisely. This is mind practice. Let's take a closer look at what mind practice means.

Mind practice refers to our efforts toward understanding the principles of the mind, and toward guarding and using the mind well based on those principles. In other words, it is the practice of disciplining our mindfulness, which is developing our attentiveness and the power of concentration. Furthermore, this development of heedfulness and focus is itself practice toward creating good and abundant results in everything we do. What this means is that the consequences of our actions manifest themselves in a way that is true to the values of ethics, practicality, and efficiency.

Often we find circumstances where ethics are present, but practicality and efficiency are lacking. There are instances where practicality exists, but there are ethical and efficiency issues. And we see occasions where efficiency is undeniable, but ethics and practicality are lacking.

Additionally, we see cases where two are present but one is absent, or one is there, but the other two are inadequate. Then there are those cases where all three are deficient or, conversely, outcomes where all three are vital.

All of these are the results of our mind's capabilities. When they mature, we produce positive results in all areas; when they are uncultivated, we create bad or trifling results. We can see innumerable cases of this reality all around us and through history.

Some peoples' lives are filled with success, others are plagued by failure, while the vast majority experience both. There are also cases in which two people undertake identical tasks under the same conditions, yet one succeeds while the other fails.

To put it another way, our successes in personal growth indicate that we have achieved perfection in using our mind, whereas our failure to grow means there was some flaw or inadequacy in using our mind.

When evaluating our mind practice, we are told to regard our successes as evidence of mindfulness and our failures as evidence of unmindfulness. Mindfulness means we have ensured the presence of the alert mind, while unmindfulness means we have failed to establish the necessary mindfulnes.

Assessment of our mindfulness offers an excellent method for developing the mind's capabilities and responding to sensory conditions in the real world. This practice can be done anywhere and at any time. It is one we can engage in when we have important business to attend to and even when we do not. By performing this practice with true intent, we can develop the qualities of mind to see the true reality. In the process, we can truly handle any of life's perceived problems because we have mastered our capabilities.

No practice is without its virtues, but there are inevitably times when practice is applicable and times when it is not, and areas where we are capable and others where we are not. Nevertheless, with this mind practice we can gain understanding and proficiency in everything we face until we finally reach a stage of complete knowledge and mastery of everything, producing grace that is without end or limit. This is the mind practice of Won-Buddhism.

Our practice ensures the highest values of practicality, ideals, and public service. Our practice is not theoretical but practical and applicable. It is not an accessory that we can do with or without. It is essential. Once we truly understand this, we cannot do without it. In addition, when we focus all our dedication on practicing steadily with a sense of purpose, our mind practice will ultimately become an integral part of our daily routine, as opposed to something we only do on special occasions.

At this stage, we must practice while working and work while practicing—our work and our practice benefit from one another. If we approach our practice this way, we gain double the advantages for half the effort.

With this method of practice, we can avoid all disasters in our life, achieve success in all endeavors, and experience ongoing progress. The effects of this extend without limitation to all areas of our lives, to every nook and corner. It is a far-reaching influence that produces unimaginable grace, enabling us to bring about loving-kindness and manifest our vision. This impact is described as "reaching even grasses and trees and extending in myriad directions."

Mind practice, according to the method of mindfulness/unmindfulness, is the most authentic, actual, effective, and practical of approaches.

Each of us has learned differently throughout eons of our past lives. Each of us has a different spiritual capacity, broadly categorized as high, intermediate, and low. When our spiritual capacity is high, we make progress effortlessly and rapidly. With intermediate spiritual capacity, it comes late and with difficulty. Those with low spiritual capacity endure a truly arduous, slow process. Finally, when we reach the ultimate stage, we experience the pleasure of the pinnacle stage without distinction. This is the bliss of the Way, and we enjoy it as an incomparable world of spiritual bliss.

To explain the levels of spiritual capacity and extent of mind practice in greater detail, it generally takes the following form, although each person will vary in maturity and tendency according to the specific conditions and components of practice:

1. Failure is virtually assured
2. Success appears likely with some effort
3. Success is guaranteed with effort
4. Success comes without great effort
5. Success comes merely from making a resolution
6. Success comes of its own accord without any resolution

Initially, these spiritual capacities manifest according to what we have learned in previous lives. After that, their placement and speed may vary depending on how much effort we exert in our practice during this lifetime.

Even though we bring these different spiritual capacities into our mind practice process, we sometimes commit the foolish mistake of failing to recognize what we have learned in past lives. Instead, we make one or two attempts, then dismiss the whole thing as impossible, stopping or abandoning our practice when success does not immediately follow. By doing this, we lose immensely and forfeit our hope for the future.

Our true nature provides a resource for mind practice and attaining buddhahood. It is not the case that each of us possesses a different nature or that some people have more of it than others. There is not even the tiniest distinction between buddhas, bodhisattvas, and all other living beings; they share the exact nature. The only difference is that buddhas and bodhisattvas have enlightened to it, whereas ordinary living things have left it abandoned and unused.

The person who practices with great zeal, saying, "I'm as capable as any buddha or bodhisattva" or "There's no reason I shouldn't be able to do that," will open the doors of even the most impenetrable of fortresses.

It is said there is no dharma outside of our true nature and no buddha outside the mind. Thus, when we seek the dharma, we must seek it in our very nature, and when we seek the buddha, we must do so within our mind. Therefore, we will find neither the dharma nor the buddha outside the mind's nature.

This mind practice is something anyone can carry out. If we truly want freedom and happiness in life, we cannot afford to ignore our minds. Mind practice allows every one of us to acquire the ability to enrich our daily lives.

So let us embark upon the path of mind practice.

CHAPTER 2

ASPECTS OF THE MIND

Before beginning mind practice, we need to have a deeper understanding of our mind. In its original sense, the word "mind" refers to three faculties: knowledge, feeling, and intention. Yet, it is not a phenomenon that can be described completely through these three simple words. Mind is so diverse, complex, and subtle, that we must examine it at a deeper level.

The Mind's Ordinary Aspect

Does the mind truly exist, and, if so, what does it look like? We must answer these questions accurately if we are to truly understand the mind.

All material things in this world have a physical form. When we encounter physical forms, we can perceive them with one or more of our physical senses. When something lacks a physical form, our physical senses cannot directly perceive it. As a result, we may lack a proper understanding of a thing or even deny its very existence.

In addition, how much do we really perceive with our five sense organs—eyes, ears, nose, mouth, and body? Even with physical phenomena, we can do little more with our eyes than see that they have an apparent form and some distinguishing characteristics. Only certain waves of light, which are visible to the human eye, are actually perceivable. Sounds, smells, flavors, textures—none of these directly create a visual perception of form. There are many things that lack sounds, smells, tastes, and textures, such as gravity, the dharma, the Way, our true nature, the essence of life, or energy. Such things are perceived not through our sense organs but through the functioning of our mind.

The actual mind itself is not something that can be perceived with our senses. Everybody has mind. It is responsible for shaping human history in all its vastness. There is really no way to discern its actual form. Mind does not have a shape that can be perceived by waves of light, so it is impossible to view it with the naked eye.

We often speak of "watching the mind" and "seeing its nature," but these phrases refer to perception through the mind's eye, not the physical eye.

When our mind's eye is open, we can see clearly without using our physical eyes.

Is there a part of the mind that can see without using the physical eyes? If there is, how does this part of the mind relate to our own physical body? These are truly baffling questions.

In any case, there are whole worlds that we will never see if our mind's eye is not open.

Sounds, tastes, smells, and the like cannot be perceived with our physical eyes, but they are perceived through the functioning of the body: our eyes, mouth, nose, and skin. They may not have shape in terms of color impressions, but they do have sounds, tastes, oders, and textures.

This is true also of the mind. It has a unique form that is completely independent of color, sound, taste, smell, and texture—it has an unpredictable and undefinable shape. We often say that facial expressions convey what is inside the mind: a smile generally means the mind is smiling, a frown means the mind is grieving, and an angry face means the mind is raging. Thus, the things that occupy our mind on a daily basis are then expressed by our face.

Facial Expressions

Let us sketch a picture of some of our facial expressions and see what it shows.

Drawing all the different aspects that appear in our mind as expressed in our faces, how much of this are we capable of showing? Naturally, the details of our picture and our methods to express them vary based on our drawing skills. No matter how great our artistic ability, it would be almost impossible to depict every expression of the mind, since it is so complex and intricate.

When judging someone's character, we may call a person "righteous" when they display many aspects of righteousness, "benevolent" when they show many aspects of benevolence, "wise" when they show many aspects of wisdom, and "humble" when they show many aspects of humility. These are all aspects of the mind. We also speak of the "Way Mountain" formed as the Way matures, the "Benevolence Mountain" formed as Benevolence matures, the "Righteousness Mountain" formed as Righteousness matures, the "Propriety Mountain" formed as proper use of the mind matures, and the "Wisdom Mountain" formed as our wisdom matures.

This is not a complete list of "Mountains." The climbing of mountains represents our spiritual ascent to enlightenment. We also say that for every ten people, the mind takes ten different forms. For every hundred, it takes on a hundred different forms. No two minds can be the same. Is it merely that sages and people of virtue have noble minds, whereas ordinary humans and other sentient beings have ordinary minds? Actually, the mind comes in a myriad of shapes and forms.

The mind's myriad aspects behave like seeds. Seeds eventually produce outcomes when they encounter the right soil. The result may be the lotus platform in heaven or the miseries of hell. In either case, the result is nothing more than the crop produced by our mind-seeds. These mind aspects become seeds that sprout into outcomes that affect us in the future. It is critical, fundamental, and indispensable that we plant our mind-seeds wisely and tend to them carefully.

The buddha who tended well to his character and ascended to the supreme pinnacle of being has both a physical body and a dharma body (Dharmakaya). The Dharmakaya is the seed of all wisdom, blessings, and grace. Therefore, what shape might it take? The possibilities are limitless.

Let us further examine different aspects of the mind.

The Mind's Linear Aspect

As it proceeds through time, our mind sketches out a line. When we walk on sand and snow, we can look back and see our footprints tracing a line. As we move without stopping, our motion creates the shape of a continuous line. Similarly our mind has a linear aspect.

The mind is never still, not for even a moment. It endlessly moves toward something or other; sometimes forward, sometimes sideways, sometimes even backward, or sometimes merely spinning in place. We call this constant motion *persistence*.

We find that there are differences that arise depending on whether we draw our line toward a meaningful place or a meaningless one; whether toward a wholesome place or an unwholesome one: and whether we are moving or not. The success or failure of our life is determined accordingly. We may leave behind footprints of greatness, footprints with no meaning, or very foolish footprints.

Such is the world of the mind's first dimension.

The path of these footsteps is a history of our life. The path maps the road that we have traveled to date. This journey is as diverse as the years in our life. Joy and agony, sadness and humor, happiness and misfortune, satisfaction and frustration, success and failure, progression and regression, advancement and retreat—all these can be found along that road.

As we look back on the road we have traveled, we sometimes do so with a satisfied smile or with a sneer of bitterness. We feel fulfillment and regret as well as pride and shame. We would like to show off the parts that make us proud and erase the parts that cause us shame. There is no erasing our past once it has been drawn. There is no retaking the steps our mind has taken. We must shoulder the responsibility for its path. No one can do that for us. It is on us.

The Mind's Planar Aspect

In addition to its linear function, our mind also has a planar function. Just as we have our ordinary notions of the *line* and *plane*, so the mind-world includes not only a linear concept but also a planar concept.

The activity of our mind is forever seeking a way to expand into new territory. As children, our interests broaden from those of a toddler to those of a teenager. Eventually, we begin to extend our attention to every place and everything in the world. We are opening not just the horizons of our physical reality, but those of the metaphysical world as well—there are no constraints.

Our mind is constantly traveling around without any discernment between the improper and the proper in the world. There are no boundaries or limitations in the worlds to which our mind travels.

As a result, we find ourselves in the world of ultimate bliss sometimes and the world of hell at other times. And we do not merely visit, we also build and inhabit these worlds of ultimate bliss and of hell.

Our mind has a function with which it opens and broadens two-dimensional horizons. When we judge people from this perspective, we say they have a mind that is "broad" or "open" or they may have a mind that is "narrow" and "closed." This view of the world is our mind's second dimension.

The Mind's Multidimensional Aspect

In addition to our mind's linear and planar aspects, it also has another multidimensional aspect. Just as we have a physical body that encompasses all things, so it is with the mind. Our mind has no physical quantity or quality, but it does have characteristic quantities and qualities in psychological terms. In addition to the spaces of reality, it also has a cyber space or a multidimensional aspect.

Minds come in various sizes. Our physical body differs in size during our infancy, our childhood, our adolescence, and our adulthood. Our minds, too, differ according to the extent of their development. As we know, there are limits to even the largest of physical bodies. In the past, people in Korea spoke of the "six-footer" as being the tallest person around. In rare cases, a person might grow taller than this, but does anyone grow over ten feet tall?

The mind is different. There are no limits to its size! We can build it up and up until its size rivals the heavens and earth. We can also shrink it down and down, until it is infinitesimally small. The mind has aspects of both the all-encompassing, leaving nothing outside, and the infinitely small, admitting nothing inside.

So, when we speak of the character of someone in this world, we might say he is a "great" person, or a "small," or foolish person. This refers not to the greatness or smallness of the physical body, but to the capacity of the mind. When *The Diamond Sutra* speaks of the Buddha's "great body," this is said to refer to the greatness of the dharma body, not the physical body. To have a great dharma body is to have greatness in this dimensional aspect of the mind.

A large mountain sustains the lives of the many creatures that live on it. Similarly, a great mind becomes a great refuge for many beings and can support many lives that come to depend on it.

This is the world of our mind's third dimension.

The Content of the Mind

Not only is our mind great, but the mind's contents are infinite. Our physical bodies are said to be made up of the five viscera and six entrails on the inside (the lungs, spleen, liver, kidneys, heart, stomach, gall bladder, small intestine, large intestine, bladder, and solar plexus) and the five sense organs on the outside (eyes, ears, nose, mouth, and skin), along with our limbs and all the cells that make up everything. Our minds, too, contain more than we could ever hope to count.

Besides its linear and planar contents, the mind also contains limitless dimensional content—incomparably more than the physical body.

It would be accurate to say that its contents are infinite. They include the negative, which is like trash, and the positive, which is like treasure. All these differ from one person to the next. No two minds have the same content. Instead, the contents are unique and so are the destinies formed by those contents. Our history, the history of humankind, is a phenomenon that appeared as those destinies combined into a single collective destiny.

We have histories of misfortune and histories of glory. If we face all this directly, if we see into its true nature, then we will understand that we cannot neglect our mind. There is nothing more urgent in this world. Our koan and our determination to solve this problem must rise high like the shining sun.

The varied aspects of our mind are often likened to a field, a sea, or a void, and other types of natural phenomenon. This shows just how difficult it is to grasp our mind, and the great diversity of all the minds that exist.

We also use a great many words to describe the mind. This comes from striving to express the diversity found in the world of mind. Our mind has an intellectual realm (knowledge), an emotional realm (feeling), and an intentional realm (will). In addition to these, we have many other words that people have coined to describe the mind: wisdom, consciousness, delusion, ignorance, benevolence, righteousness, humility, arrogance, joy, anger, sadness, pleasure, love, mercy, fear, desire, conscience, hatred, hope, and so on.

The scriptures and canons of the world's religions were developed around the mind, illuminating the path that it should take. Even the vast stores of texts that we have, like the *Tripitaka Koreana*, are just a sliver of this world of mind, its unlimited nature, its endlessness and inexhaustibility. At the same time, our mind-world contains within it, without exception, all infinite arcane principles, infinite treasures, and infinite creative transformations.

The Mind Is Like a Tree

A tree has roots and a base, a trunk, and branches. So, too, does our mind. We live rooted in a home with our family, and the tree lives rooted in the earth. The mind, too, has a place in which it is rooted. A tree's branches are rooted in its trunk, the trunk in its base, the base in its roots, and the roots in the ground. So, too, is the volitional mind rooted in the emotional mind, the emotional mind in the intellectual mind, the intellectual mind in the nature, and the nature in the truth.

The truth spreads through and embraces all things in the universe. Depending on our cultural background and orientation, we may use different terms to refer to the truth. We may call it Heaven, Allah, God, Jehovah, Dharmakaya Buddha, Shangdi, the Way, or Wuji, "the ultimateless." While these terms may differ, their true nature and essence are the same.

Just as the essence of water does not change, even when each culture uses a different word to refer to its form.

Both terms and their interpretations may vary, depending on the extent of our intellectual understanding of water or of cultural differences. Interpretations may differ very much indeed, according to the environmental circumstances surrounding water or the perspective and emotions of the person gazing on it. The perspective of the scientist will not be the same as that of the poet.

This is critical to our understanding of the original nature and the truth. We do not express and interpret the truth differently because of any differences in its nature. Rather, our relationship with the truth is like the proverbial blind men examining the elephant. The one who feels its belly will say it is like a wall, the one who feels its legs will say it is like a pillar, and the one who feels its trunk will say it is like a great serpent.

So, we use different expressions, hold different views, and make different claims according to our views of the nature of truth, the aspects of it that we have seen, and the level of our understanding. But if you tell this to the person who has seen it in its entirety, he will simply nod his head and say, "It is all the same."

Those who have failed to see the whole will fixate on their own opinion and reject any others. They will debate who is right or wrong. Their argument will intensify until they eventually divide the world into a bloody battle between "us" and "them." This is what has been observed so many times in human history and among the religions of the world.

While the truth may be interpreted in different ways depending on our intellectual abilities and the extent of our awakening, nothing changes its true nature. It is, simply, just as it is and spontaneous. It is not present or absent depending on the views that a person holds, nor is it something that can be either this way or that way.

At the same time, the truth is spread throughout all phenomena in the universe. It embraces everything without exception, and all things in the universe are rooted in it. Nothing in this world exists without it.

This is true for our minds, as well. Just as the tree is rooted in the ground, our mind is rooted in the nature of truth. Our mind also forms roots and a base, a trunk and branches. Once we understand this, we will be able to develop and cultivate the rootless tree. Let us examine this a bit more closely, observing the way in which the mind functions.

CHAPTER 3

THE MIND'S CONTENT AND SCOPE

Truth, Our True Nature, Consciousness, Feeling, and Intention

(1) Truth

I explained before about the nature of truth. However, it is not something that can be described in a few lines of text. It would be difficult for us to understand it using all the words in all the languages of the world. Yet at the same time, it can be expressed fully through the simple words, "The cypress tree in the courtyard."

Not only is it the realm where no words are necessary, it is also one which cannot be reached by using any word. The reality of the mind is the realm where words have ceased. And yet this realm embraces everything in the world: nothing left behind, no corner untouched, no place unaffected by the function of its creative transformation.

The words used to describe this indescribable truth-realm include Wuji, The Way, True Nature, Shangdi, Dharmakaya Buddha, Heaven, Allah, and God. Different terms have been used depending upon the cultural context and perspective of the person viewing the realm, but true nature is always the same.

Like the soil where plants put down their roots, this realm is where our 'True Nature' takes root. In *The Golden Mean*, it is described as, "What Heaven commands is our Original Nature." These words may be interpreted in a number of ways. Heaven, or the Truth-Realm has "commanded," "determined," "ordered," or "bestowed" our original nature. All of these phrases express the same reality, so each is correct.

This describes the Heavenly Realm of Truth as the direct source of our original nature. Just as every business and household is served by a municipal water system and every plant is rooted to the earth, everyone's Nature taps into the truth-realm, sharing equally in its benefits.

All of these benefits are realized through the natural principle of non-action, with no fabrication or concept intruding on them. As a result, it is impossible to explain them fully using language created by humans. The only way to comprehend them is through contemplation.

Therefore, rooted in Truth, our original nature is the root of all discriminating mind-states. This includes thoughts, knowledge, perceptions, emotions, feelings, intentions, and so forth. Once the discriminating mind-states take root, they work together, giving rise to our will.

Since our nature makes up the foundation for knowledge, feeling, and will, and we refer to this as the realm of the mind.

Let us take a closer look at this Nature and the world of knowledge, feeling, and intention.

(2) Our True Nature

Although they generally agree on the existence of our original nature, Eastern and Western philosophies differ greatly in their understanding of it. These differences have been the topic of fierce debate over the years. Since our true nature has no form, sound or smell, the philosophers' interpretations have diverged based on the knowledge and perspective of each viewer. We cannot discuss all of them here, but I would like to pick some typical examples of Eastern and Western thought and look at their primary perspectives.

First, there are those who claim that human nature is inherently bad.

Leading proponents of this view include Sun-tzu in the East and Thomas Hobbes in the West. In Sun-tzu's view, it it is obvious that human nature is fundamentally evil. "Human nature is bad," he wrote. "Goodness is nothing more than a falsehood. From birth, it is the nature of the human being to love gain and to show no restraint in seeking it. We are foolish and wicked from birth, and we become cruel and greedy as a result. We experience physical desires from birth, leading us to feel carnal desires as we pursue them."

Meanwhile, Hobbes argued that humans are intrinsically selfish. Therefore, the natural condition of humankind is where everyone is the enemy of everyone else. For this reason, he said, social constraints are necessary to protect mankind from it's own natural impulses.

The opposing argument states that we humans have an inherently good and decent nature.

In the East, this position is championed by Zisi, while Jean-Jacques Rousseau is a representative proponent in the West.

Zisi said that our true nature is conferred on mankind by the Heavens. Thus, human nature is no different from the way of heaven and must be good. Gongsun Chou noted that everyone possesses a mind of compassion, a mind of shame, and a mind of restraint. He cites this as proof of our inherently good nature, one of benevolence, righteousness, propriety, and wisdom. Thus, in these views there is no need to question the goodness of human nature. All that is required is to recognize this Nature and follow its way.

In the West, Rousseau shared this view.

Since our human nature is inherently good, Rousseau argued, it is right to give ourselves the freedom to follow our nature, and bad to restrict that freedom. The core of Rousseau's thought was a call for us to "return to nature." Immanuel Kant argued this same point from another angle. He proposed that we are endowed with practical reason, which he viewed as having the character of moral principle. He said that autonomy and freedom come when we follow our practical reasoning. In this way, he voiced the view that humans are good by nature.

There is also an alternative to these opposing views. Kao-tzu in the East and John Locke in the West refused to characterize Mankind as either innately good or bad.

He described our nature as being like water. Just as water flows to the east when its path travels to the east and flows to the west when its path travels to the west, our nature tends to become evil when our environment draws us to evil and good when it draws us to goodness. Based on this, he argued that there is no good or bad in human nature.

Locke holds a similar view on the influence of the environment on our nature. He describes it in terms of a blank slate or "Tabula Rasa." Just as words are written on the page, our mind acquires representations through experience. The content of an individual's character is simply a matter of whether they encounter more representations of good or more representations of evil. In other words, good and evil are simply products of the experiences that we acquire in life.

In his commentary on *The Doctrine of the Mean*, Zhu Xi wrote that our mind is, by nature, nothing more than pure awareness. The appearance of differences between the human mind and the Way mind stems from the different mind states that emerge from the personal body and from the foundation of right human nature and destiny. Even the wise man of high spiritual capacity must have a human mind, even the foolish man of low spiritual capacity must have the mind of the Way. Both wise man and fool are obliged to govern these minds well. This view forms the foundation of Neo-Confucianism.

Other theories on human nature have also been proclaimed by the established religions, but none of them strays very far from the argument that we are inherently decent as human beings.

We should refer to the message as articulated by Won-Buddhism. Won-Buddhism holds that a person's nature is expressed in both quiescence as well as action. This means that we may be without either good or evil and yet capable of doing either good or evil, depending upon our actions or inaction. This is the true face of the phenomenal world that we experience countless times over the course of history. All human history draws a dual curve of good and evil. The important and urgent matter is managing our human nature.

In other words, the various elements contained in our nature contain limitless potential. How we manage and use these elements is the core issue throughout the history of our human civilization and will continue to be a matter of life and death in the future. To examine how we can best manage these elements, let us take a look at the world of knowledge, which is rooted in our nature.

(3) Consciousness

"Consciousness" refers to "knowing," but it is distinct as a concept from the mind in the strictest sense because it also contains the meaning of the sub-conscious. The word "mind" refers to the state in which thoughts or emotions have emerged from its ground. When describing consciousness, we casually use these words synonymously. For this reason, there are many words in Korea that include the Chinese character for "consciousness," or *sik* (識): understanding (*chisik*), discernment (*kyŏnsik*), recognition (*insik*), and karmic consciousness (*ŏpsik*). A similar character is *chi* (知), meaning "to know," as well as *chi* (智) meaning "wisdom." This latter character is made up of the *chi* meaning "to know," together with a symbol representing "the sun" or "day" (日) underneath. Thus, it is a "brighter" concept of knowledge than the ordinary *chi*. In addition, there are many similar words relating to consciousness, but all of them refer to or share the concept of "ultimate knowledge."

In philosophy, this concept of "knowing" is called the *episteme*, and the exploration of knowledge is called *epistemology*. In epistemology, there are two major theories of what makes up our "knowing." One theory holds that all "knowing" is based on experience derived from the senses, whereas the other claims that all knowledge is constructed from reason alone, independent of any particular experience. These opposing views have resulted in two schools of epistemological thought: The Empiricists who regard knowledge as experiential or "a posteriori" in nature and the Rationalist who regard knowledge as innate or "a priori" in nature. In Buddhism, the doctrine of "Mind Only" has attempted to precisely investigate both schools of thought. In the process, it has created a thorough analysis by delving into the deepest realms through a specialized theory unlike any utilized in the past. I will explain the essence of it here.

Buddhism describes human experience and knowledge in terms of the six sensory conditions, the six sense objects, the six sense organs, and the six consciousnesses.

The six sensory conditions are how we perceive our environment: what we see with our eyes, hear with our ears, smell with our nose, taste with our mouth and tongue, detect through contact with our body, and that which we can distinguish with our consciousness.

We use the term "six sense objects" to describe the expressions of each of these conditions: colors, sounds, smells, tastes, sensations, and thoughts. The six sense organs refer to eyes, ears, nose, tongue, body, and mind.

Then there are the six consciousnesses: eye consciousness, ear consciousness, nose consciousness, tongue consciousness, body consciousness, and mind consciousness. These various states of consciousnesses arise as the six sense objects encounter the six sense organs. A presence exists that oversees all these states of consciousness. It is called the seventh *manas* consciousness. There is also an eighth, *alaya* consciousness formed from the spilling over of the *manas* consciousness. The ninth *amala* consciousness encompasses all of these. One might think of the seventh *manas* consciousness as the storage tank for memory and consciousness experience, the eighth *alaya* consciousness as the storage tank for the deep sub-consciousness, and the ninth *amala* consciousness as the root that encompasses all of these. In other words, we can easily understand the seventh consciousness as the discriminating mind, the eighth as the spirit, and the ninth as the realm of our True Nature.

This explains the structure of our consciousness and how karma is shaped as countless six sense objects enter through the gateway of the six sense organs. It is a truly staggering insight and a statement of truth, just as it is.

Therefore, once we understand these principles, practitioners must not waste time, but instead direct our focus on the task of purifying our unconscious and subconscious worlds, for the seeds stored there will be revealed outside of our consciousness. When we have greed, anger, and delusion stored in our mind; greed, anger, and delusion will arise from our consciousness. When our mind stores precepts, meditation, and wisdom, they arise from our consciousness. In other words, when defilements are stored, defilements arise. When the seed of awakening is stored, enlightenment will arise. Defilements are hard at work establishing hellish states, while awakening seeds work diligently, creating lotus platforms in the world of ultimate bliss.

How can we see this just as it is and not postpone the purification of our conscious and unconsciousness worlds? We must be busy, busy, busy in our practice.

(4) Feeling

Our knowledge eventually summons forth feeling. "Feeling" refers to the world of emotion that arises from the mind's contact with objects. The knowledge that forms through the six sense organs and six consciousnesses is not the final product of that interaction. We also experience feelings based on that knowledge. We call these our "impressions," our "likes" and "dislikes." When we become caught up in these impressions, we call them our "emotions."

We divide this world of feeling into seven types: joy, anger, sadness, fear, love, hate, and desire. We can have joyful minds, angry minds, sad minds, fearful minds, loving minds, hateful minds, and desirous minds.

While it is possible to separate out these seven main types, there are obviously many, many more.

Buddhism describes nine types of sentient being's minds: embryo-born, egg-born, moisture-born, metamorphosis-born, with form, without form, with thoughts, without thoughts, and neither without nor with thoughts. In truth, there is no limit to the different types of sentient beings' minds. The number of minds that arise when we encounter objects is greater than all the grains of sand in the Ganges River. The Chinese characters that represents these minds all bear the radical meaning "mind", (忄) and anyone who speaks a language with these characters knows that they are very many indeed. Greater still is the number of the words made with those characters. All of this represents our struggle to show just a single aspect of the mind-world. Even if we were to use every one of these words to express it, we could not describe the whole of the mind-world's true nature.

However, in summary, the mind is composed of two stages: The stage of consciousness [both sik (識) and chi (知)] and the stage of knowledge. There is another level of the mind's operation beyond this stage, called the world of intention.

(5) Intention

The mind experiences feelings from contact with objects, based on inherent knowledge and enters the realm of Intention distinct from knowledge and feeling. Beyond simply "wanting to do," Intention refers to a state where the mind has begun operating. Feelings lead to the formation and expression of a goal. Intention is quite active and deliberate.

For example, when we see someone suffering, knowledge forms, and we experience the emotional sense of "How awful." This is feeling. When we have the mind to help them, that is intention.

Understanding, or will are other words for Intention. What emerges from *intention* is the motivating force for our vows, our determinations, our questioning, our pursuits, and our efforts to accept our goals. This force is how we face the affairs of the world.

Thus, feeling comes from knowledge and intention comes from feeling. In turn, intention gives rise to action. In turn, action forms new knowledge, which builds up and gives rise to more feeling, which produces stronger intention, which leads to the next action. As this cycle repeats and repeats, we form a more powerful and active consciousness.

This active consciousness grips us with a powerful force and does with us as it will. This marks a crossroad, with one path leading toward good karma and the other toward bad karma, depending on whether the cycle is a virtuous or vicious one.

A virtuous cycle is a cycle of corresponding to life-giving action, while a vicious cycle is one of corresponding to harm. They turn and turn to shape the myriad forms and phenomena: suffering and happiness, prosperity and poverty, success and failure, progression and regression. The core premise is that the intention of our first and second cycles must be based on virtue. Otherwise, we will be unable to escape the cycle of evil destinies. When the core premise of "goodness" is firm and unswerving, the result is a virtuous cycle that produces limitless grace. Should selfishness, perversity, or evil intrude, the result is a vicious cycle that produces limitless harm, bringing great disaster upon ourselves and others.

Once we understand this principle, we understand that we must cultivate the Way and practice great repentance. As our practice of great repentance and cultivation of the Way reaches its pinnacle, we reach a stage where there is no mark of transgression to be found inside, outside, or anywhere. We must reach this stage before we can rest easy about ourselves.

(6) Other Elements

I have provided a general picture of the way in which our mind is rooted in the truth and connected with our true nature, feeling, and intention. But this is only a rough outline. If we venture inside its truth, we find a limitless world that cannot be fully described and explained in words. We call this the "system of the trichiliocosm" though this phrase is also inadequate to truly describe that limitless realm.

Sages and spiritual masters have been shedding light on this mind-world from many different perspectives for ages. Here, I would like to single out some perspectives that are particularly illuminating. Understand that this mind-world is beyond all powers of expression, so a great many frames of reference and interpretations are possible depending upon one's viewpoint. Our methods of application may also differ widely. Keep this in mind at all times.

In Eastern Philosophy, the principle behind the universe's formation is interpreted in terms of *yin*, *yang*, and the five primary elements (metal, wood, water, fire, and earth). In this metaphysical framework, the phenomena of this universe is understood to be shaped through the intermingling of the five energies according to the cycling of *yin* and *yang*. When these energies come together with corresponding life-giving, they revive us with new vitality; when they come together with corresponding harm, they lead to destruction, and ultimately extinction.

This framework of the five elements and Yin/Yang forms the basis of everything from Eastern medicine and philosophy to the study of mind-nature. Even our moral character arises from a connection with the five elements of the Universe: We form a Benevolent nature from wood energy, Propriety from fire energy, a Faithful nature from earth energy, a Wise nature from water energy, and a Righteous nature from metal energy.

In Confucianism, there is something called the four beginnings: the 'Compassionate Mind' is said to be the beginning of benevolence, the 'Mind of Shame' the beginning of righteousness, the 'Mind of Humility' the beginning of propriety, and the 'Mind of Forbearance' the beginning of wisdom. According to this view, all of us inherently possess minds of benevolence, righteousness, propriety, and wisdom.

In Christianity, our conscience is said to be the voice of God. When we follow our conscience, we are obeying God's will. In this way, God is present within us. Therefore, every mind that has a conscience is understood to embody the will and mind of God, while the mind that is based in wickedness is understood to embody the mind of Satan, which the conscience must overcome.

Buddhism describes two main types of minds: the Mind of Defilement and the Mind of Awakening. The Mind of Defilement grounds itself on a foundation of misleading ideas and the three mental poisons: greed, hatred, and delusion. The Mind of Awakening grounds itself on a foundation of buddha nature. A Mind of Defilement drives us to cycle through the triple evil world of animals, hungry ghosts, and hell. A Mind of Awakening guides us to enlightenment and liberation.

Defilements come in 108 types, centered on ten principal evil actions: three involving the body (murder, theft, and adultery), four involving the tongue (abuse, idle talk, lying, and slander), as well as the three mental poisons. We are encouraged to exert ourselves and accumulate merit to drive them away. The mind of supreme enlightenment can be centered on the Threefold Practice of precepts, meditation, and wisdom, or on the Eightfold Path (right view, right intention, right speech, right action, right livelihood, right effort, right mindfulness, and right concentration) or the six pāramitās (generosity, morality, forbearance, diligence, concentration, and insight). We are told to use these to overcome the ten evil actions and the 108 defilements.

In addition, each religion sets its own precepts and instructs us to guard against negative elements within our character. Christians uphold the Ten Commandments. Buddhist practitioners heed the five precepts for lay followers, the ten precepts for bodhisattvas, and the 250 precepts and 500 precepts for monastics. In Won-Buddhism, we have a total of thirty precepts: ten for the ordinary grade, ten for the grade of special faith, and ten for the grade of the battle between dharma and Mara. These precepts include guidelines for speech, action, and the mind, but those having to do with the mind receive special emphasis and are considered to be the most fundamental.

Each religion also designates positive elements that can be found within the human character, as its articles of faith. In Christianity, they are Faith, Hope, and Charity; in Cheondoism: Sincerity, Reverence, and Faith. Confucianism designates its articles of faith in three groups: The Guiding Principles of Allegiance, Filial piety, and Fidelity; The Five Relationships of Father-Son, Ruler-Subject, Husband-Wife, Elder-Younger, and Friend-Friend; The Five Constant Virtues of Benevolence, Righteousness, Propriety, Wisdom, and Fidelity. In Buddhism, we are taught to take refuge in the three jewels of the Buddha, Dharma, and Sangha and to enrich these in our practice with the four great vows of the bodhisattva (Sentient beings are numberless. We vow to save them; Delusions are endless. We vow to eliminate them; Teachings are infinite. We vow to learn them; Supreme enlightenment is inconceivable. We vow to attain it.). The Articles of Faith from these religions represent different frameworks that guide us to maximize the positive elements within our mind.

Despite the different expressions used from one religion to the next—Christianity speaks of love, Confucianism of benevolence, Buddhism of loving-kindness—the goal and foundation are one in the same.

Spirit, Energy, Matter, and the Mind

I have sketched a general picture of the activities within our mind. Now I would like to examine our relationship with the matters around us that center on the mind. First, we will look at spirit, energy, and matter and their relationship to the mind.

All physical matter in the phenomenal world is described in terms of being solid, liquid, or gas. If we are playing the game of "20 Questions," we would start with "animal, vegetable, or mineral." These categories classify the world according to the material aspect of all beings. But this matter cannot exist without spirit or energy. Indeed, the three main components that make up this world are spirit, energy, and matter. What is the relationship among these three things? And what is their connection to animals, vegetables, and minerals?

Spirit is ever-bright and ever-numinous, it is the agent (*alaya* consciousness) that contains all consciousness. Energy is the driving force that enables all action. Matter is the framework that holds spirit and energy.

None of these three things can exist separately from the other. Indeed, the universe itself is composed of all three. Each thing that manifests in the universe arises from aspects and actions of these components. Thus, nothing exists separately from spirit, energy, and matter. We may view the universe as a numinous body or a body of energy or a physical body, based on whether we observe it from a spiritual perspective, an energy-centered perspective, or a material perspective.

We can also say that spirit is either present or absent, or that energy is present or absent. Matter is what we see and encounter directly, so we do not have any exact theory about it. Still, several conjectures remain for the others. Let us examine this more closely.

First, we need a deep understanding of what is meant by the word *hold*. Picture a bale of cotton. If it were to fall into the river, the water would hold the cotton. At this point, the water is the "primary," so to speak, and the cotton's movement is determined by the circumstances of the water. Now, let us suppose that the cotton has been soaked with the water. In this case, it is now the cotton that holds the water; the cotton is the "primary." And the water must now follow whatever happens to the cotton.

In animals, spirit holds energy and matter. In vegetables, energy holds spirit and matter. In the case of inanimate objects, the matter contains spirit and energy. In no case do either spirit, energy, or matter exist without the others. Even dung has its spirit and energy. When it encounters the right circumstances, its spirit, energy, and matter all work together. After all, a plant flourishes when we nourish it with manure. This is proof that even dung contains vibrant energy. And this is certainly true for all objects that exist in this world.

All objects have specific spirits that form the characteristics of that object. All objects have a 'Being Spirit.' Living things also have a 'Life Spirit.' Animals have a 'Sense Spirit' in addition to their 'Being and

Life Spirits.'

The manifestation of Spirits that compose an object is dynamic. Their presence within an object may change under different circumstances. For example, when we are in a deep sleep or under anesthesia, only our life-spirit remains. While only our life-spirit is present, we do not feel pain. A person who is undergoing surgery under anesthesia doesn't feel a thing even when his entire body is being cut open. Only after the sense-spirit has revived does he feel the pain. Higher animals possess a larger portion of Sense Spirit whereas lower animals possess less.

Human beings represent a more developed form of animal. We will find differences between the spiritual capacity of a person with a dominant Sense Spirit and a person living with dominant Life Spirit. A person who has reached the ultimate in the Sense Spirit is called a "sage" or "buddha." The more we are dominated by the 'Life Spirit,' the more instinctive we become; the more we tend toward the 'Sense Spirit,' the more creative we become. The 'Life Spirit' and the 'Being Spirit' are passive. The 'Sense Spirit' is active. 'Sense Spirit' enables the agent that is the mind to rise and control all our different thoughts and actions.

Importantly, spirit commands energy in order to transform matter. Energy causes actions to transform various material things based on the dictates of spirit. Matter embraces both spirit and energy, while spirit commands energy to control and minister matter.

To express this phenomenon in another way, we may say that "the marvelous existence of true suchness has filled the dharma realm"; that "the great wisdom of prajna penetrates the ten directions"; and that "there is no object that does not conform to the profound principle, and living creatures are sheltered by the shade of its loving-kindness." None of the myriad objects in this universe can escape, even slightly, from the principle of spirit, energy, and matter.

Our practice gives us the strength to hold our ground in terms of the *spirit*, *energy*, and *matter*. By making effective use of these and carrying them out in tandem, we can create a synergistic effect, which produces twice the result with half the effort.

Therefore, we need to take steps to purify our spirit. We must eliminate any atmosphere that might taint our spirit. We should create an environment where our spirit can be purified. We must also recognize both the harmful and beneficial nature of objects our spirit encounters and act accordingly. Stay away from sensory conditions and objects that pollute, and take steps to frequently encounter and be influenced by environments and objects that purify our spirit.

As the saying goes, if you lie down with dogs, you wake up with fleas. Our spirit is influenced by what is nearby. A polluted spirit is toxic and brings harm to both ourselves and those around us. A pure spirit fosters a flourishing life force and produces grace wherever it goes.

Water has a strong life force depending upon its purity. Clean water has an energetic life force that brings limitless grace wherever it goes. Conversely, tainted water loses its vitality, and becomes toxic, bringing harm wherever it goes.

Whether we have a clean or tainted spirit commanding our energy and body, is of crucial importance. It is the crossroad to either committing transgressions or creating blessings. We have no choice but to focus on our wisdom and our dedication to minister our spirit, energy, and body.

Among the three elements, spirit occupies the center. Its functioning is linked to our mind. The functioning of our mind links to the spirit. There it is stored and expresses itself as the mind, again and again.

Whether this cycle is a virtuous cycle or a vicious cycle determines our destiny. A virtuous cycle is a cycle of purification, while a vicious cycle is a cycle of pollution. When we enter a virtuous cycle, our spirit becomes more and more clear. Its vitality grows without limit. But the more we repeat a vicious cycle, the more our spirit is diminished and we lose our vitality. Poison harms us and others.

From this principle, we can easily deduce the necessity of cultivating the spirit. Once we understand this principle, we cannot fail to engage in Cultivating the Spirit, for this is crucial to our very future and destiny.

What, then, is the connection between the spirit and the physical body?

Some very interesting questions arise here. How does spirit connect to the physical body? Is there a specific principle that determines the soul's conception? If so, what principle does the process follow?

Let us look at this more closely.

Principles of the Soul and Body

(1) The Universal Spirit and Individual Spirits

As we continue our discussion of the soul, let us first examine the relationship between the universal spirit and individual spirits.

The Buddhist idea of "consciousness only" states that all objects are only the manifestation of our thoughts. The "mind only" doctrine posits that the essence of all phenomena in the universe is the spirit. As this suggests, there is a spiritual nature that exists as a void reality behind the world and all its phenomena. So mysterious, numinous, and perspicacious is the essence of this nature that we call it "eternally empty and aware."

Those whose wisdom is open, sees into it like a jewel in their hand. When wisdom is clouded, one can live in the middle of the spiritual world and see nothing at all.

In a sense, the universe is simply a mass of spiritual nature. Every tangible object in the universe is just a creation of the spiritual nature based on its principles. This nature is: exceedingly radiant; exceedingly meticulous, just, proper and natural; vast and immeasurable; eternal and imperishable; without either good or ill fortune; free of thoughts. It is also a mass of purity itself, without a shred of error, a hint of mistake, a speck of difference mixed in. This great mass is called the *universal spirit*, and it fills all things in the universe in equal measure. There is no place or object that it does not penetrate. Just as we are endowed with a spirit in our body, so the name of "universal spirit" is given to the spirit of the whole universe.

It is not merely present; it performs the workings of formation, duration, decay, and emptiness in the universe; at the same time it performs the workings of birth, old age, sickness, and death of all things. It truly is something of unfathomable mystery.

Let us now look at the principle by which individual spirits are derived from this universal spirit.

In my previous explanation of the spirit, I mentioned the being-spirit, life-spirit, and sense-spirit. All of these are based in the universal spirit and shared by everything that exists in this world. All objects have an additional Being Spirit. All living things have an additional Life Spirit. All animals have an additional Sense Spirit. Humans have another special Sense Spirit. Moreover we as humans have other specific spirits added to our shared attributes. As we move deeper into each person's individuality, we find yet other special spirits added on. We sustain ourselves as the universal spirit and individual spirit operating together.

It has been conjectured that this may have something to do with biology and DNA. I don't possess any specialized knowledge about biology, so I will limit my explanation to what I have outlined here and address the issue solely as a koan.

As the content decreases, scope increases, and content increases as scope shrinks. More content means smaller scope and less content means larger scope.

Therefore, the individual spirit cannot exist separately from the universal spirit, and the universal spirit cannot exist without the individual spirit. The universal spirit exists together with the individual spirit and the individual spirit exists together with the universal spirit. The person who does not understand this believes the individual spirit and universal spirit to be separate. The person who understands, knows that the individual spirit exists within the universal spirit and that the universal spirit is joined with the individual spirit.

The universal spirit and individual spirit exist together and every clump of grass, every insect, and every object falls within this world.

The universal spirit has a world of principle that follows the universal spirit and the individual spirit has a world of principle that follows the individual spirit. "World of principle" refers to the world of the principles that become the foundation of objects. Based on their respective principles, the universal spirit functions as the universal spirit, while the individual spirit functions as the individual spirit, creating and transforming this universe and the myriad things in it. Once we have understood the principle of progression from the individual spirit to the universal spirit, we have understood that "all dharmas return to one." And once we have understood the principle of progression from the universal spirit to individual spirit, we have understood the phrase "to what does the one return?" I will now provide a more concrete explanation of this principle by separating it as the principle of division.

(2) The Principle of Combination and Division

There exists in this world a fundamental principle, by which all the worlds of phenomena are created. Every clump of grass and insect arises and disappears according to this principle. It is all too apparent that we humans cannot be born or die in the absence of this principle. We do not simply arise and disappear without order, without principles or rules. It is an arising and ceasing that occurs within an orderly principle. Every situation that unfolds in the world of phenomena is merely a product that arises from the twisting and turning of this principle. What is expressed on the outside is merely the final phenomenon; underneath its surface, countless workings of this principle have taken place in order to bring it into being.

This principle includes both metaphysical and physical principles. It also includes principles of combination, which apply to all things, and principle of division, which applies only to a single part.

All these principles are interwoven with each other, forming the entire universe and every last object in it.

Among the Dharma Words, there is one passage that reads, "When a huge circle (*Wonsang*) turns, thousands and tens of thousands of smaller circles (*Wonsang*) turn accordingly, just as small wheels of a machine turn as its motor turns."

When things are applied in ways according to this principle, we call them "proper" and "rational." When they go against this principle, we say that they are "improper" and "irrational."

To treat things properly and rationally is not only wise; it produces the intended outcome as well. When we treat things improperly or irrationally, and our actions are foolish, this gives rise to an outcome that runs counter to what was intended.

We humans have achieved scientific advancements by applying principles of physics and advancements in philosophy and religion by applying principles of metaphysics.

The principle of combination is the formative principle of the universal and fundamental. The principle of division is the formative principle of the individual and the particular. Within these principles, the whole and the individual maintain an organic interconnection. The universe and the myriad phenomena in it are sustained by them through their mysterious operation. No object or form can exist outside of this principle.

So, how does the principle applies to our birth and death as human beings? How does that principle apply to the human being in the womb? Theory of prenatal education must be founded on a proper understanding of the unborn human being and the principle of truth that relates to life and death.

We human beings begin as fetuses, are born into the world, and then live out our lives before eventually dying. This process from conception and birth to death is a progression that we experience directly. Something we see takes place in countless instances all around us. Everyone is aware of it, but few perceive a profound understanding of death and the process of conception and birth. Such an understanding may be beyond the reach of human intelligence. This should not be taken as the absence of a principle of truth.

The facts of truth have no dependency whatsoever with what we know and do not know. Truth is always only brightness and clarity.

These days, we assume that we have achieved advancements in our intelligence as human beings, yet what we do not know is limitless, especially compared to what we do know.

It is very foolish to behave arrogantly because we mistakenly believe that the firefly glimmer of knowledge we possess with the vast sea of this great universe somehow represents something extraordinary. However ignorant we may be, there is unquestionably a principle of truth that includes death, conception, and birth. The question is: "What principle serves as the basis for its operation?" Let's start solving this riddle, by contemplating the following questions:

1. What kind of relationship exists between the soul and the body? Do they exist together with death, or separately from it?
2. Are death and conception discontinuous or connected? Is there a cycle of samsara that leads from conception to birth, life, death, and back to conception?
3. Do conception, birth, life, and death have an influence over the next process? As we answer these questions, prenatal education's principle will become clear.

(3) The Soul and the Body

The Soul has been the subject of a great debate over the entire course of human history.

Of course, we have the central question of whether human beings have a soul or not. The debate does not end there even among those who agree on its existence. There has always been disagreement regarding the nature of the Soul. Views differ according to historical currents, cultural perspectives, as well as our scientific knowledge and philosophic perspectives.

All these points of view have existed as two major currents, according to the general philosophical trends that emerged as science developed in the modern age: the Materialistic perspective and the Spiritual perspective. The materialist perspective denies the existence of an independent soul.

Scientists in the former Soviet Union hypothesized that spiritual workings were the result of laser beams. They tried and failed to prove this through scientific experimentation, attempts that were funded with enormous amounts of money from national coffers. Not only were they unsuccessful, they ended up proving that no one could do anything about the facts of the truth. This came at the same time the Soviet Union was developing methods of spiritual therapy.

Meanwhile, many scientists in the United States studied matters of the soul. They even published their work openly and organized conferences on the subject. Their findings have received formal recognition. The research team of Dr. Ian Stevenson at the University of Virginia spent years working in this area, drawing the recognition of the American Association for the Advancement of Science. They have also studied the relationship between present and past lives, presenting case studies in a book called *Children Who Remember Previous Lives*.

In addition, there was also an account of an eye disease suffered by Edgar Cayce. He saw hundreds of previous lives while undergoing memory regression hypnosis. He visited the places mentioned to verify the details, elucidating principles that apply to life and death.

These were compiled in a book called *Many Mansions: The Edgar Cayce Story on Reincarnation*.

Other examples include Koto Ben's *World After Death*, as well as a veritable torrent of books investigating Emerson's law compensation. Elisabeth Kubler-Ross, a former professor of psychiatry at the University of Chicago, affirmed based on her study that death was merely a process of shedding this skin. This, she said, was not something that she "believed," but something that she deduced from research and examination. She said that she was 100% certain of this, and that it was not a matter of "believing" or "not believing."

So even the scientific community, which previously took a dismissive view on the existence of the soul, has now moved toward actively affirming it.

Another perspective is one that affirms the existence of the soul from the outset. This is the position voiced by the various religions of the world. But all of them differ in their opinions and perspectives on the existence of the soul. East and West, ancient and modern—every religion makes different claims. I will avoid making any specific reference to these individual perspectives, and merely focus on the position of Buddhism, which has gone into the matter of the soul in great detail.

In the early days, there were no sages or religions that provided detailed accounts of the soul as did Sakyamuni Buddha. The Buddha thoroughly investigated the mystery of the soul. But this understanding was not readily adopted by the world, resulting in many misunderstandings about Buddhism. Many people follow different religions today, and they may disregard the Buddha's insight into the soul, yet the truth is unchanging.

It seems that as science has advanced in recent years, the principles delineated by Buddhism are being borne out. Science has relegated the doctrines of primitive religions to the status of mythology and children's stories. The core principles Buddhism have been examined have proven true by science.

Many materialists and people in general have rigid confidence in their view of the soul. They deny everything beside what they themselves know, and their attitude can be one of blind and uncompromising rejection. The doctrine of Buddhism can be neither simple nor shallow.

After achieving full awakening to the truth, the Founding Master Sotaesan looked at the scriptures of Buddhism and said, "The teaching of the buddhadharma is the supreme Way of all under heaven. It illuminates the principle of true Nature, solves the crucial matter of birth and death, elucidates the principle of cause and effect, commands the paths of practice, and thus surpasses many religious doctrines." It is a truly wondrous thing that Buddhism illuminated this truth of the soul and solved the matter of birth and death.

So, let us now examine the matter of the soul as described by Buddhism and connect it to the fundamental issue of prenatal education.

Buddhism describes the body and the soul from different angles. The body arises from the combination of the four great elements: earth, water, fire, and wind. When we die, these elements scatter once again, returning to earth, water, fire, and wind. Our soul, on the other hand, takes on a new life again according to the karma we have created. We cycle through the three time-periods of past, present, and future. Although our body and soul are separated in death, a person who has acquired freedom of the soul through cultivation of the Way is capable of freely separating and combining the two.

We know of early dharma masters, who separated and combined body and soul. In Korea, we are familiar with the monk Jinmuk, who is known to have done this. The body is a phenomenon akin to an illusion, it is a bubble in the water, a shadow. The soul is the essence of the subjective ego.

When viewed from the standpoint of the soul, which represents the True Nature of the subjective self, life and death are based on the same foundation. Thus, the Dharma Words of the first section of Chapter Nine on "Sending on Spirits in Transition" in *The Scripture of The Founding Master* read, "Only a person who dies well can have a good rebirth and a good life in the next, and only a person who has a good birth and life in the present can have a good death." This is a concise summation of the truth of birth and death.

To offer another illustration, a plant's strength when it first sprouts determines how it grows. The shoot that is strong from the beginning will continue to grow in a healthy way. The shoot that is feeble from its beginning will be feeble and slow in its growth. The strong and healthy plant will bear perfect fruit. The only perfect fruit is that which blossoms from a plant that has grown well as the result of the right nutrients, moisture, and sunlight and has avoided the ravages of insects.

In contrast, the plant that receives insufficient nutrients or sunlight during its growth or suffers the attacks of insects will never bear perfect fruit. When we sow seeds from the perfect fruit that forms through a normal growth process, a healthy sprout will emerge. Conversely, when we sow seeds from poor fruit that develops through an abnormal growth process, the shoots that emerge will be very feeble indeed. It is a cyclical process: from seeds to shoots, growth, and fruition, with the resulting seeds sown in turn to develop into their own shoots. The present process necessarily influences the one that follows.

This is an example of the above principle—that we must be born well to live well, we must live well to die well, and we must die well to be reborn well—being applied to the biological body.

When we experience our death, our water substance (such as the blood that exists within our body) returns to water energy; our earth substance (our bones, for example) returns to earth energy; our fire substance (our warmth) returns to fire energy; and our wind substance (the content of our breathing) returns to wind energy. However, the way that we lived our life is reflected and condensed in our soul and when we receive a new body based on the corresponding affinities, we see this as our conception or birth.

Each of us must live well to be able to well prepare for our death. Only the well prepared soul can live a fulfilled life.

If a problem arises with any one process, it becomes a seed that leads to trouble in the next process. For this reason, we must continue working to address the factors that cause defects in each and every process.

We describe this effort as "cultivation of the Way" and "mind practice." The procedures that we undertake with our conception, prenatal care, education, as well as the various rituals that we carry out from those of birth to those after death, are all part of our effort to minimize the causes of defects and promote the causes of strengths based on the principle of the spirit.

The balanced combination of our spiritual self and our physical self will lead to a fulfilled life. The spiritual aspects of our life influence our physical life and vice versa. They intermingle in a profound relationship. The soul is the master and the body is the servant. The soul is the foundation. How we support and nourish our spiritual life will determine the kind of life we live.

(4) The Numinous Consciousness's Path to Conception

The original foundation of the spirit is the Nature. The foundation of the Nature is the Void, which admits no intrusion by physical or philosophical concepts. "Latency" forms in the spirit through the effect of repeated encounters with the six sensory conditions from outside (those of our eyes, ears, nose, tongue, body, and mind) and the functioning of our six sense organs (our eyes, ears, nose, tongue, body, and mind).

We also call this "karma." Expressed in terms of Buddhist scholarship, the six consciousnesses form through the repeated influence of the six sensory conditions and the actions of the six sense organs. A seventh consciousness (*manas* consciousness or *manas-vijnana*) forms based on the impact of these six consciousnesses and an eighth consciousness (*alaya* consciousness or *alaya-vijnana*) forms based on the intensity of the seventh consciousness.

The seventh *manas* consciousness (*manas-vijnana*) stores memory consciousness, while the eighth *alaya* consciousness stores latent consciousness. Memory consciousness belongs to the body and latent consciousness to the spirit. While the body's memory consciousness may be extinguished with the death of the body, the spirit's latent consciousness is not extinguished even after the body dies. Rather, it lies dormant in the spirit, playing a crucial role in the process of our receiving a next life, and relentlessly exerting unconscious action.

The soul and the condition of our spirit are critical factors in determining our next life. Also, the extent of practice contributes a great deal as well. The defects and strengths of our character will sprout, grow flowers and bear fruit in the ground of our next life. They prosper in good conditions, and they wither in bad conditions. Conditions conducive to defects are not good for strengths. Conditions good for strengths are bad for defects. This is true.

A final factor: All things of this world have the property of seeking to find and unite with like things. This is true for substance, but it is even more true for energy, and still more for the spirit. So, when the soul is roaming in the spirit realm searching its destination, it strikes home like an arrow when it encounters an environment that fits with what is stored in the spirit. This is what we call the union of soul and body—the conception of a new life.

Viewed in terms of this principle, prenatal education becomes essential and indispensable. Prenatal education begins with preparations for the receipt of a new soul. It is a question of whether the spirit will be one of greed, anger, and delusion or one of loving-kindness, wisdom, and charity. When the home environment is filled with greed, anger, and delusion, the spirit that arrives will be filled with greed, anger, and delusion; when the home environment is filled with loving-kindness, wisdom, and charity, it will greet a spirit replete with loving-kindness, wisdom, and charity. Even with the occasional exception, affinity for like things influences the union of soul and body above all other factors.

Prenatal education is therefore something we should already be doing on a regular basis. Even after the spirit has been invested, we need to take steps according to the properties of the strengths harbored within that spirit. This is prenatal education. Whether it is the defects or the strengths that gain power is a matter of the utmost importance. Once weeds gain hold, grain cannot flourish. Conversely, when grain flourishes, weeds cannot survive.

Cultivation is essential, and prenatal education means properly cultivating the numinous consciousness. When we do a good job of cultivating the strengths in the numinous consciousness, our prenatal education is successful.

This is why proper prenatal education requires us to maintain a right mind, be cautious with our words, behave well with no deviation in our conduct, and avoid even the slightest recklessness of emotion.

We must be particularly aware that the fetus receives all things through the mother: nutrients, oxygen, even the perception of cold, hot, cool, and warmth. Emotions of joy, anger, sadness, fear, love, hate, and desire are received through the mother, as is the awareness of the principle to practice through repeated action.

There are said to be three circuits of exchange between mother and fetus: psychological, physical, and behavioral. The mother's conduct with her body and mind is communicated directly to the fetus through these three channels. A child's growth and educational outcome are influenced by the mother's conduct in psychological, physical, and behavioral terms.

Thus, mother's every action of mind and body, and all the things she experiences from the outside, function as education of the greatest importance for the fetus. This is the essence of prenatal education.

As I was writing this section, a Won-Buddhist came by to pay her respects. She came holding a baby who was just a few months old, and she told me something very important. From the time when she was first pregnant with the child up until it was born, she would get up at four every morning to pray for the baby. And after the baby was born, it woke up every morning at exactly four o'clock.

Even the time that a baby rises in the morning is influenced by the actions of its mother.

The Mind and the Workings of Cause and Effect

In the preceding sections, I have provided a general explanation on the relationship among mind, soul, and body. Let us examine the connection between our mind and the workings of cause and effect.

Everything in this world has a cause behind its functioning—a cause that necessarily produces effects, these produce new causes in turn. This rule cannot escape the metaphysical realm or the physical realm.

All phenomena are simply the outcome that arises from a boundless set of causes. Any change that occurs in our reality is the result of the cyclical functioning of cause and effect. Sometimes, the results are like great mountains. Other times, they are like great mountains crumbling away.

The mountains may have good outcomes or bad ones. It is an ironclad rule that good outcomes come from good causes and bad outcomes from bad causes. When the cyclical repetition of cause and effect proceeds toward what is correspondingly life-giving, the outcomes are good; when it proceeds toward corresponding harm, the outcomes are bad. This is the indisputable truth of cause and effect.

In his sutras, Sakyamuni Buddha describes how we receive transgressions and blessings based on this principle of cause and effect as we act with our body, words, and intentions. We find these descriptions in the *Sutra on the Retribution of Sins and Merits*, the *Sutra on the Variety of Karmic Rewards*, and the *Discourse on the Five Blessings of the Benevolent and Wise*.

In these sutras, the Buddha tells us that "if I were to try to speak of all the things for which sentient beings receive transgression, it would pain my heart too much." He also teaches that, "All the heavens will afford the kindest of treatment when we do ongoing acts of grace for others with the spirit, body, and matter; the myriad evils will all recede and all the minions of Mara will be extinguished, so that there will be none who dare defy us." Finally, he relates the feeling of seeing into the principle of cause and effect: "Seeing with my wisdom eye the receipt of transgressions and blessings from countless eons ago until I received this body now is like seeing a glass bead in the palm of my hand, its inside and outside crystal clear, leaving not the smallest hair of doubt."

With this in mind, what are the properties of the principle of cause and effect?

The vicissitudes of fortunes and misfortunes, the calamity and happiness of life—rising and falling, prosperity and decline, benefit and harm, gains and losses suffering and happiness, prosperity and poverty, success and failure, transgression and non-transgression, blessing and non-blessing—none of these happen outside the principle of cause and effect.

Thus, the giver becomes the receiver and the receiver the giver. Benefit comes from the right, harm from the wrong.

The person doing something has a role to play, but there is no part for he who does nothing.

Opportunities are given to those who diligently prepare; no opportunity is given to those who neglect to make any preparations.

What has been given is taken away when we behave recklessly. Blessings come in response to life-giving and humility. Disaster comes in response to harm and arrogance.

There is a principle that states all is given where we dedicate all. And another principle that affirms, only lonely resentment results when we keep things to ourselves.

When we do good works, good things happen for us and for others. When our deeds are bad, bad things happen not only to us but to others as well.

The wise approach, then, is to solve all problems of reality in a way that fits these principles of cause and effect—prepare, plan and take steps for the future. To simply hope for a windfall, reflects a truly foolish mind. One will eventually experience an outcome of great failure. Successful outcomes that build great mountains or bring failures that bring great mountains crumbling down, are simply a matter of cause and effect.

As monumental as the outcome of cause and effect may be, at the heart of it is the seed of mind. The mover within the mind draws on energy to generate the functioning of our six sense organs, creating the form of the cause. Once that cause reaches a certain level, it generates an effect.

The things stored up in our mind can be either weapons of harm or they can be the arms of grace. When we see this properly, it can be said that we have seen the Nature. To put it differently, what we store in our mind may be either a positive cause or a negative one.

For this reason, we must constantly clear away the negative causes and endlessly promote the positive ones through mind practice and cultivation of the Way. I will describe the negative and positive causes in more detail in the section on defilements and great enlightenment. For now, you should give deep consideration to the fact that negative causes are the seed of all misfortune and positive causes are the seed of all merit and happiness.

We often see people seeking fortune in external things. They believe that misfortune comes from the outside, and so they may perform rituals to ward off evil. These are nothing more than the flailing efforts of those who fail to understand the principle of cause and effect. Others search through fortunetelling or the reading of facial features. Still others search in gravesites and horoscopes. All these efforts are in vain in reality. Nothing can defy the principle of cause and effect.

The book Ma Yi's *Appearance Method* as has been described as the "Bible of Physiognomy." The forward of this book addresses predicting a person's future destiny. It states that the four pillars (the year, month, day, and time) are not the same as physiognomy and physiognomy is not the same as the mind image. Destiny is found in the mind image—that is, in the mind itself.

There is a Chinese saying: "When sincerity is in the heart, it takes shape on the outside." This tells us that what lies at the center of our mind is ultimately expressed through our face, our words, and our actions.

Furthermore, all our other possessions—our health, wisdom,

fortune, knowledge, honors, status, rights, affinities, and so forth—behave in accordance with our mind. When our mind is coarse and without virtue, we use our possessions coarsely and without virtue.

Once we use our possessions, a corresponding outcome is sure to follow. That effect, in turn, functions as a new cause, leading us to new action. And the repetition of that action leads, finally, to the formation of karma. That karma then takes control of us and holds us in its sway.

More precisely, the actor inside us becomes nothing more than a slave to karma. Our actor is placed under its thumb. As a result, we find ourselves engaging in all manner of works and evil deeds, doing things we would never imagine, without any hesitation. In the process, the chain of karma tightens relentlessly around us. We lose any hope of escape as we are caught in an endless chain of samsara.

We need to have a deeper and more accurate understanding of karma. I will describe it in detail in the pages to come. For now, I will say that the mind lies at the center of it all. The mind always commands cause and effect. Therefore, we must establish and reestablish how important the management of the mind is, and take this fact deeply to heart.

The Mind, Karma, and Samsara

We act according to what is in our mind and our karma takes shape according to how we repeat those actions. The arising karma becomes the driving force for samsara. We must have a proper understanding of what is meant here by "karma." Indeed, all these actions result in tremendous force as they bind together.

The Earth was created when specks of dust, powerless by themselves, came together as a whole. What a tremendous force of gravity the Earth now possesses! Everything in this world depends on the Earth and it holds firm. Indeed, it embraces and gives life to all. In this way, even the tiniest of things can exhibit great power when they come together. Toilet paper, for example, is flimsy by itself, but I have experienced how difficult it is to tear, when it has been wound into a roll. And this is not true only for things with form. Air has no form, but when it comes together, as a tornado, it exhibits the awesome force of a bombshell.

The same is true for our mind. Any kind of mind can exert a force beyond our imagination when it binds together. Good forces result when good minds come together. Bad forces take shape when bad minds come together.

We have often seen how many individual minds filled with

resentment come together and cause great calamities. Human minds bound together in resentment can bring down a government or leave a country in ruin. Thus, the leader of every country, every group, every organization, indeed every position of leadership, should unite good minds and prevent bad minds from binding together, if he is to be a wise leader and bring hope.

The collective bundles that are formulated when we use our six sense organs make up our karma. Although unseen, they possess a fearsome force. This force can be a power for great aspiration for vengeance, or it can become a power for spiritual discipline. When it is a power for spiritual discipline, it may develop into strength for spiritual cultivation, growth of wisdom and observation of the precepts. It may be good karma or bad karma. Good karma has the power to lead us through the cycle of good destinies, while bad karma has the power to cause us to cycle through unwholesome destinies. Together, they create numerous destinies of forms and phenomena.

We must give deep thought to the *power* described here. With power, there is a world of esoteric principles. In fact, some people take the view that power is the original source of all things in the universe. In the East, power is classified as two energies (*yin* and *yang*) and the energies of the five elements (metal, wood, water, fire, and earth). These serve as the basis for understanding all the principles of formation. Based on these principles, the medicinal properties of herbs have been discovered and applied to treatment. This is called "using medicine in response to the disease."

Everything, be it physical, psychological, or behavioral, comes together to create a force when bound together. Even specks of dust clinging to pillars of a mill and black spots on the base of a pot possess amazing medicinal powers.

In this way, karma represents the accumulation of things shaped by the body, mouth, and will. This bundle grows through repeated action, building up even greater strength. Even ordinary metal becomes a magnet when you rub it repeatedly in the same direction with another magnet, producing a force that draws other metals closer together.

We often say that people have become addicted to alcohol, drugs, or gambling. These addictions represent karma formed through repeated action. Once karma has formed, it exerts a powerful influence over us. We become its slave, and it orders us around like a servant. Our actor has no freedom or sovereignty. We merely do as we are told. We are led to cycle through good destinies when it is good karma, and evil destinies when it is bad karma.

What we need to realize here is the absolute importance of not committing the original transgression. By original transgression, I am referring to when we go astray at the very beginning. Once we make a poor start, one mistake will follow another. But when we start out properly, everything that follows will be more correct.

Thus the beginning is of utmost importance, and what makes the decisions at this stage is the agent lurking in our unconscious world. As I mentioned earlier, when talking about consciousnesses, the expression of the content stored up in our seventh or eighth consciousness becomes the mover, dictating all action. And that action creates new karma, which is stored in its turn within the seventh or eighth consciousness before finding expression based on that state.

The term we use to describe this is samsara.

The fateful question that determines the destiny of this actor is whether an awakening or defilement is stored in the seventh and eighth consciousnesses. We must effectively control those moments when they find expression from these consciousnesses. If we alter our course to a virtuous cycle, it summons the power of that aspiration and imposes itself forcefully against any expression of wrong content so that the darkness in our future will lift and brightness will open. This is the way to escape from our transmigration into unwholesome destinies.

This may seem like a tall order, but this is a world where we see clearly when our wisdom is open. It is something that all living creatures experience and re-experience constantly. It is not far away or removed from us at all.

Our mind produces actions; those actions form karma through our body, words, and intentions. That karma then produces samsara, taking hold of us and forcing us to repeat the same actions. In this way, the mind lies at the heart of samsara, controlling everything. Therefore we need to have a complete understanding of the importance of managing the mind.

The Mind
: Paths of Progression and Regression

Various class systems operate in our society. Public servants in Korea start out at Level 9 and progress to Level 1. In the military, people start out as privates and advance to become officers, field officers, generals, and so forth. Classes are not confined to administrative hierarchies. In professional fields, people are classified into levels and groups based on their abilities, receiving credentials of "a certain rank" or "such-and-such group" depending on how their abilities get rated. When we ascend, it is called advancement and it is called demotion when we descend.

Human beings like to move upward and hate to move downward. The mind is at the heart of all our upward and downward movement. Whether it is competence in our conduct, competence in our professional field, or capability in any area at all, the functioning of our mind is at the center.

In other words, the mind causes progression or regression. This is an issue in our social and professional realms, to be sure, but it is even more the case when it comes to the realm of spiritual capability. In the past, the different religions would use rank and the title indicates a person's degree of moral maturity. Confucianism classified knowledge into stages of "innate knowledge," "knowledge from learning," and "knowledge through difficulties," and actions into stages of "action based on pleasure," "action based on comfort," and "action out of compulsion." In Buddhism, there are the sravaka (hearer or disciple), the pratyeka-buddha (solitary buddha), the bodhisattva, and the buddha, or the four fruits of the Stream-entrant, the Once-to-be-reborn, the Non-returner, and the Arhat.

In Won-Buddhism, we have the ordinary grade, the grade of special faith, grade of the battle between dharma and Mara, the status of dharma strong and Mara defeated, the status of beyond the household, and the status of the greatly enlightened. We will not go into detail about these ranks here, but the criteria for determining them are the strength of our mind abilities and the rigor of our efforts. Without the mind, then, this hierarchy could not exist.

In a religion, we devote tremendous effort to exertions and the accumulation of merit, staking our very lives on them so that we might enter a world of higher mind capabilities. The person who sets out on the road to progression will live a life replete with limitless satisfaction and joy, while the person who sets out on the road to regression will regret it and regard it as a great misfortune. Not only will each person perceive their choices in this way, but their reality will bear out their perception. The person who opens the road of progression will walk a path of glory, merits, and happiness, as opposed to the path of mortification and suffering tread by the person who opens the road of regression.

Here, too, the mind lies at the center of these two extremes. When we use the mind well, the road to progression is opened, and when we use the mind poorly, the road to regression is opened. Section 25 of the chapter on "Cause and Effect" in *The Scripture of The Founding Master* provides a description of the progressing mind and the regressing mind. "Those in the period of progression," it reads, "have a good and gentle nature, do not harm others, and harmonize well with whomever they encounter; always advocating humility, they extol others and love to learn; in particular, they have faith in the truth, strive in their spiritual practice, wish others to do well, and by any means possible encourage the weak. Those in the period of regression, by contrast, are vicious by nature, cannot benefit many people, and conflict with whomever they encounter; being arrogant, they like to look down on others and do not like to learn; in particular, they have no faith in the truth of cause and effect and do not engage in spiritual practice; and they cannot bear to see others do well, trying by any means possible to cut down others who are better than themselves."

Again, all living creatures aspire to progress and hate to regress. Again, the solution must be sought in the mind.

The Mind, Self-Cultivation, and Developing World Peace

The first of the four major books of Confucianism, *The Great Learning* is studied by those who plan to cultivate their personal life, regulate their household, govern a country, and keep the world at peace.

The book consists of three objectives and eight steps. The three objectives are "illuminating the lucid virtue," "renewing the multitude," and "stopping at the utmost goodness." The eight steps are "studying the things of the world," "achieving knowledge," "sincerely executing the will," "righting the mind," "cultivating the self," "governing the home," "governing the country," and "bringing peace to the world."

Though the ultimate goal is national rule and peace throughout the world, proper control and practice with the mind comes first.

The book's tenth chapter on the proper government of the state and establishment of a peaceful world, tells us that "the minister should have a single mind; even if he has no other talents, he should have a beautiful mind possessed of all-embracing generosity; enjoy the talents of others like his own; and, when he sees the benevolence and nobility of others, he embraces them truly with his heart, and not simply through his words. Such a person is capable of summoning benefits that bring about security for posterity and the masses. But if he envies the talents of others, despises them, refuses to engage with them out of opposition to their benevolence and nobility, and lacks generosity, he may fail to ensure the security of the masses and even threaten their future."

In other words, our character and the use of our mind can preserve a country, or it can trigger its collapse. Everything, self-cultivation, even household management, state administration, and the preservation of peace in the world, is determined by the way we use our mind.

The collapse of a house collapses is preceded by the collapse of the minds of its members. The collapse of a country is preceded by the collapse of the minds of its citizens and leaders. No group can survive when the mind collapses.

If we examine the instances where the mind collapses, we find that it results from distrust, greed, sloth, arrogance, and delusion. Truth collapses, faith collapses, rational wisdom collapses, the mind of dedication collapses, and the mind of unity collapses. Once the mind collapses, real-world problems cannot be successfully resolved. We will not even succeed in safeguarding those things that we already have. Ultimately, all will be lost. Conversely, the home, society, the state, and the world survive and great historical achievements are made, when the mind survives.

The mind truly is a great thing. When we use it well, there is nothing we cannot do. The well-used mind can achieve anything. The question remains of how to illuminate it properly—how to cultivate it and use it well.

Most people have not formed a sense of working toward the mind's discovery and illumination, cultivation, and effective application. We see it push outward toward the fringes of modern civilization, where it lies neglected. The case for questioning that I give you now is, "Can we truly afford to leave the mind off in a corner, neglected?"

> *With the way—good fortune—the one hundred blessings return.*
> *Without the way—ill fortune—the one hundred calamities befall us.*

The Mind and Health

What is the relationship between the mind and health? Is health merely a matter of the physical body? Once we have lost our health, everything from that point on belongs to the mind. When the mind shows no consideration for health, no medical treatment is possible. There are steps that we take for the sake of treatment, and activities that we must abstain from completely. All of these necessarily require the consideration by the mind. Because of this necessity, none of them will succeed without the presence of the mind. Every kind of treatment, whether drug therapy, music therapy, or exercise therapy, requires the mind to be enlisted if it is to succeed.

Almost anyone can recognize that our health depends on the mind. What influence does the mind have on health? Earlier, I gave a brief explanation about the spirit, energy, and substance. Spirit is the foundation for energy and substance, exerting an effect on them; energy influences spirit and substance; and substance influences energy and spirit. We experience the turbulence and vicissitudes of life as these three elements exert their effects on one another. Issues of health must likewise involve spirit, energy, and substance.

These days, we see a lot of neurological diseases, ailments that are associated directly with the mind. When our nerves weaken, we experience sleep disorders. As the ailment worsens, we may find ourselves suffering from mental problems, unable to perform the normal functions of a human being. Of course, the cause sometimes lies in the body. But whatever the cause, it ultimately manifests itself as a pathological phenomenon of the mind.

Furthermore, we find the prefix "neuro-" attached to the names of all these kinds of diseases of the body. There are all sorts of medical terms like this: gastraneuria, neurogastritis, neuroenteritis. In such cases, a precondition for treatment is that we establish peace of mind. The treatment will either be slow to work or fail to work if our mind is not at ease.

In Eastern medicine, diseases are explained as stemming from external causes (wind, cold, heat, and moisture) and internal causes, which include the seven emotional factors of joy, anger, melancholy, worry, grief, fear, and fright. An excess of any one emotional factor causes damage to our viscera, and this ultimately manifests as disease.

In general the effects of the emotional factors are as follows:

Joy is emotional activity of the heart. In excess, it results in the consumption of mind energy, leaving us with an uneasy body and mind and affecting the functions of the lungs.

Anger is an emotional activity associated with the liver. In excess, it harms the blood as energy rises upward, consuming *yin* and blood and causing fire energy to flourish in the liver.

Melancholy is closely associated with the lungs. Since the lungs control energy, excessive melancholy leads to blockage of lung energy. The symptoms that may result include frustration and despair.

Worry reflects the emotions of the spleen. Too much mental

concentration or contemplation is said to be harmful to the spleen.

Grief reflects the emotions in the lungs. Too much grief can impair the functions of the five viscera and is also said to lead to disease by harming the "three burners," or the upper, middle, and lower *jiao*.

Fear is a reflection of kidney emotions. Excessive fear is said to harm kidney functioning and leads to terror and anxiety.

Fright refers to emotional anxiety caused when spiritual energy becomes disordered by a sudden stimulus from an outside object.

As you can see, the energy-based diseases of Oriental medicine are ailments that stem from the mind. The mind and health are thus closely connected. Furthermore, when we tally up all the influences on our health—diet, exercise and other medical concerns or common sense—we can see that the mind truly does lie at the heart of our health management.

That is not all. Even in dire situations like cancer, we find cases where people hold out and beat their disease. We also see many instances of completely healthy people ruining their health by cursing themselves with pessimism about their lot in life. The mind must serve as a watchdog for health. To be more precise, we must awaken more deeply to the fact that the health of the body is predicated on the health of the mind.

Nevertheless, most people these days seem to be in a situation of great distress resulting from the diseased state of their very minds. This is becoming a major social issue. Sotaesan, the Founding Master of Won-Buddhism, said the following about the mind-disease we suffer today in the 34th section of the "Doctrine" chapter in *The Scripture of The Founding Master*: "In today's world, the further civilization advances externally, the deeper the source of illness becomes internally, so that we will soon fall into a terminal state unless we do something about it. This must worry people who are concerned about the morality of the world."

In the same section, he went on to say that the illnesses in question are the illnesses of money, the illness of resentment, the illness of dependency, the illness of a reluctance to learn, the illness of a reluctance to teach, and the illness of a lack of public spirit. To treat these illnesses, he says that we "must first promote the study of the Way, that is: The Way of being content with one's lot in life; the Way of discovering grace at its very source; the Way of leading a life of self-power; the Way of learning; the Way of teaching; and the Way of leading a life for public benefit. Through such teaching, each person should look internally at oneself and treat one's own diseased states of mind."

He also provided information about other key illnesses. It is beyond question that the number of illnesses that emerge within each of our minds is far greater than this. Just as there are countless diseases that afflict the body, the diseases of the mind are too numerous to count. Indeed, it would be correct to say that there are more of them than there are diseases of the body.

These illnesses of the mind eventually lead to illnesses of the body and illnesses of society, tormenting and threatening our very lives. We must therefore take to heart the understanding that health of the body can only be assured when our mind is healthy.

Defilements and Great Enlightenment

So far, I have given a few general examples of areas associated with our mind. In truth, however, there is nothing in human affairs or human civilization that is not connected or associated with the mind.

Indeed, the mind lies at the heart of all these things and plays a pivotal role in everything. At this point, the meaning of the words "all things are created by the mind" should strike the reader with their profundity. Only when we have awakened to this principle, will we have had a taste of what it means to see into our true nature.

For this reason, we need to take a deeper and broader look at the mind-world. When we look inside this world, we see numberless minds, minds without end. They are as numerous as the grains of sands in the Ganges River, so to speak.

These minds may constitute numerous forms, but we can in essence, classify them into positive minds or negative minds. Positive minds are called *awakening minds*, while negative minds are called defilements. We can also express the idea of awakening "dharma," and defilements as "Mara."

The positive mind is the mind of the Way rooted in our true nature, awakening, and in the dharma. Whereas the negative mind is the human mind rooted in the physical body, defilements, and Mara.

The world of our mind is one in which the elements of a proper character are mixed with those of an improper character. As practitioners, shall we leave that mixture of minds as it is or manage it, and put it in order?

We need to answer this important question.

First, look at the negative aspects of mind that form one strand of our mind-world. The mind that we do not want.

All religions make their own references to this, but allow me to start by discussing Buddhism, which provides an in-depth analysis. In Buddhism, defilement is considered the opposite of awakening. There are said to be 108 types of defilements. To estimate the amount of these defilements, we first multiply the defilements that arise from our six sense organs—those we see with the eyes, hear with the ears, smell with the nose, taste with the tongue, feel with the body, and think or feel with the mind—by the three types of feeling: suffering, pleasure, and the realm of neither suffering nor pleasure. These 18 defilements are then multiplied by the two types that emerge in from the realm of desire or lack of desire. Those 36 defilements again are multiplied by the three time-periods of past, present and future, giving us a total of 108 defilements. In the sense that practitioners purify 108 defilements, we turn each of the 108 meditation beads one at a time while reciting the buddha's name.

There are living creature worlds formed through these defilements. Numbering nine in total, they are referred to as the nine forms of living beings.

Those nine types are those born from fetuses, those born from eggs, those born from moisture, those born from metamorphosis, those with form, those without form, those with thoughts, those without thoughts, and those neither with nor without thoughts. To expand on this a bit, the four births (fetuses, eggs, moisture, and metamorphosis) represent creatures that live by instinct (the life-spirit). The creatures of form are those that emphasize the reality of right and wrong, gain and loss. The world of those without form is one that emphasizes the pursuit of an ideal world. For those with thoughts, it is a world that emphasizes the perspective of a religious sect that learns and teaches. For those without thoughts, it is a world that emphasizes the position of Zen sects in which the human mind is accessed directly without dissertation. And those living creatures that are neither with nor without thoughts represent a world that avoids being hindered by either of these things.

The four forms of birth mentioned above are described as the worlds of living creatures of birth, while the remaining five are the living creatures of thought. Together, they are called the nine forms of sentient beings. Nine forms are listed here, but this is nothing more than a classification for convenience's sake. In truth, it is more correct to say that living creatures are without number or boundary.

At the heart of these defilements and the world of sentient beings, there are the three mental poisons (greed, anger, and delusion) and the misleading notions: the idea of ego entity, the idea of a person, the idea of sentient beings, and the idea of long life. These create all sorts of defilements, and form sentient being minds. As a result of this, the negative elements in our mind's character are continually erupting, and ceaselessly tormenting us and everyone around us.

The figure who commands all these minds is known as "Papiyan, the king of the Maras." He is forever leading an invasion against positive minds, using a vast array of tactics, never hesitating to use the most extraordinary methods. Doing so, he leaves our minds with a very difficult plight indeed. These defilements represent the hired soldiers and the drugs of Papiyan.

If we examine the attributes of Mara's minions, we find that:

Mara's minions are constantly lurking on the path of practitioners of the Way, using guerrilla warfare tactics against them while drugs paralyze the spirit and leave them in a state of confusion.

Mara's minions become allies when conquered, but enemy forces when they are not vanquished.

Mara's minions weaken before the strong and become a mighty force against the weak.

Mara's minions seek to conquer us by tempting and seducing us into places of pleasure and fixation, and they thrive even more in places of dislike and hatred.

Mara's minions seek out and dig into weaknesses but withdraw from places of perfection.

Mara's minions seduce us with favorable conditions, dissolving our mind away, and they torment us with adverse conditions, leading us to succumb to resignation.

Mara's minions are experts at disguise, but they withdraw once detected. If left undetected, they idle away, holding out and thriving even more.

Mara's minions detest places of equanimity, fairness, and justice. They enjoy discriminating minds, negative emotion, and places which are perverse and selfish.

When we are awakened, even defilements awake. But when we fail to achieve awakening, they become minions of Mara, and even our six sense organs become their mercenaries.

All responsibility for the actions of our six sense organs, once they have become mercenary soldiers of Mara's minions, ends up returning to haunt us.

Wisdom and good fortune in our future come when we do not allow ourselves to be swayed by these minions of Mara.

The single most pressing concern for the practitioner is whether we subjugate or are subjugated by Mara's minions.

Mara's minions will not guide us to ultimate bliss. Rather, they forever block the way to ultimate bliss, using all sorts of temptations and torment to guide us into hell and an array of unwholesome destinies.

So, we need to have an accurate understanding of the nature of these minions. We must monitor them closely so that they cannot lurk inside us and make a sport of us. There is a term that is used in police investigations: "the target is under surveillance." This is said when someone requires careful monitoring because of the risk that he will commit a crime. Mara's minions are targets that we cannot leave unmonitored for even a moment. We need to keep them under constant surveillance, so that there is nowhere for them to hide and they will be unable to exert their force. This is the reality of defilements, their true nature and substance.

Let us now turn our attention to *bodhi* or awakening. Awakening refers to a mind that functions as a positive influence within our character. This is not simplistic wisdom that corresponds to other forms of conceptual thought. Awakening is the living embodiment of all positive and moral concepts associated with good character.

In other words, *bodhi* or awakening is the opposite of defilement. While defilements represent things that we must abandon, *bodhi* or awakening is something that we must embrace. Defilements create greater harm when they increase, yet *bodhi* brings greater fortune and more abundance. While defilements lead us to disaster, *bodhi* guides us to prosperity and well-being.

The sages of religions that have existed throughout history came forth to alert us to the way we are controlled by defilements, to develop wholesome and ethical norms, and provided a philosophy for us to follow.

I have merely given the most important items here. The *Tripitaka* and the so-called "five cartloads of scriptures" all represent teachings aimed at producing this great enlightenment. Each of them carries pearls of accumulated wisdom and loving-kindness to rescue us from unwholesome destinies and guide us toward paradise.

When the dharma words of these teachings dissolve into our mind, the kith and kin of great enlightenment assemble into an armies, leaving the minions of Mara with nowhere to stand. And the world of the buddha and bodhisattva unfolds into a glorious vista.

Part II
Principles of Spiritual Cultivation

CHAPTER 4

What Kind of Object is the Mind?

Based on what our mind holds inside, and everything that is outside of it, what should we be doing with our mind? Can we leave it unattended, or is the mind something that we need to manage thoroughly? And if we do need to manage it, how do we do that? What rules and methods should we apply? These are questions in need of answers.

In order to drive a car, we need to learn how to do it and then we need to practice. And this is certainly true of many other things, not just cars. Everything we do and use in this world has aspects that we must learn. The person who understands this principle and prepares thoroughly will live wisely in this world. The person who fails to realize this, and neglects the steps of preparation, will lead a careless life full of difficulties.

Can we disregard a mind that is always at the center of our experience? This mind that we cannot live apart from for even one minute? The mind that we must use endlessly? Can we ignore it or leave it to its own devices? This is something that requires serious consideration. In the past, many sages, and wise men and women, inquired about this continually. People today tend to live superficially without ever questioning the nature of the mind. Even those who show an interest never look deeply enough, but dwell instead at the superficial level.

Let us ask the question: What is the nature of our mind? We need to establish a general sense of direction when we ask this question. Although this is not a course in inquiry that can answer these questions completely in just a few words, I hope we can at least provide hope for the future as we establish a direction for our questioning.

Something to Be Sought

In our lives, we experience loss and deprivation. We suffer failure and great hardship as a result. This is because we have lost or have been deprived of our mind.

The Korean people are intimately acquainted with the pain of deprivation. We have had much experience with having things taken away from us in the history of our nation. The terrible suffering of having our sovereignty stripped away for 36 years of rule by the Japanese empire is something that can never be forgotten. It remains at the core of the heart of every Korean. The perpetrators have no experience of that suffering. They dismiss it—at most they may say, "I guess it probably hurt a bit." However, those who suffered the pain cannot dismiss it. The experience remains a deep wound.

The price of deprivation is steep. Therefore, we feel compelled to regain whatever has been taken from us. We feel that we must get it back, whatever it takes. Koreans recovered their lost sovereignty when the country was liberated. As a result, we developed our country into one of the world's top ten economies in just a few decades. Now, our children grow up in comfort, laughing, crying, and playing to their hearts' content in their own country, their own land. How proud and happy a sight it is! Kim Koo, a freedom fighter who fought for the independence of Korea once said, "For my country, my people, I am even happy to be slapped in the face."

When we have had something taken away, must we reclaim it? What we do with it when we recover it is a subsequent question. If we can recover it, we have the freedom, the right, and the opportunity to resolve whatever follows.

We can easily recognize the loss of material things, but we fail to recognize when we are living our lives deprived of our mind. Few of us even try to reclaim our mind. Instead, each of us finds ourselves living our life with our mind stolen from us. Who does the mind belong to, anyway? It is ours. It belongs to each one of us. Yet, we still live with our minds taken away from us by external sensory conditions. This is what Francis Bacon called the "idols of the theater."

Our minds are taken away from us by the sensory conditions of desire, joy, torment, fondness, contempt and every other favorable or adverse sensory condition. Sensory conditions steal our sovereignty— our control of our minds are squashed by them. This is the state of the mind governing the secular world. This is the wretched existence of a living creature in samsara.

As a perfect example of this, let us examine the way in which our minds and souls have become slaves to money in the modern era. As a society, when money tells us to steal, we steal. When money directs us to corruption, we follow. When money tells us to speak ill of others, we do. We will say that something evil is right when money tells us to do so. And we call even right things wrong when money says we should do so. Astonishingly, we have even seen people committing murder for money without any hesitation when instructed to kill.

This how our mind becomes a slave to money, and how our sovereignty crumbles: we are then unable to be free. Our sovereignty is utterly stripped from us, yet we fail to realize it. Money gives its orders, and we simply nod and say, "Yes, yes." We are left numb by the pleasures of flattery given to us in exchange. Colonizers have always been careful to flatter those from whom they have taken everything. Once we have succumbed to flattery and indulgence, we live in ignorance, and it becomes exceedingly difficult to break free from that bondage. You may well dismiss this account as extreme, but if you look closely into the reality of today, you will see that this is not an overstatement. Indeed, it is sometimes more severe than this.

We live our lives having forgotten, lost, or having been deprived of our mind. Yet, we do not even think to reclaim it. Can we afford to leave this condition unattended?

When we have lost a material thing or had it stolen, it is nothing more than a portion of our possessions. This is not true for the mind. When our mind is lost or taken from us, we have lost everything. Unlike the loss of things, which are limited to themselves, being stripped of the mind is a deprivation of our foundation. The all-encompassing nature of this loss is of a higher order. The scope of the damage is incomparable. If we cannot see this, then we truly have no hope of breaking free from the misfortune of samsara.

Therefore, we need to regain possession of the mind we have lost or had taken from us. The fact that we work hard to recover our money and objects, yet we do not recognize when we have lost control of our mind, nor try to reclaim it, is a major problem for us.

There are so many things that we can do once we find our mind, and nothing at all we can do when we do not have it. Not only is it gone, but we become the slave of the thief who stole it. We then live as its puppet. What an awful fate! Yet, once we have recovered our mind, we can freely and inexhaustibly become the creator of truly remarkable ideas.

Our mind, then, is the one thing we need to keep and preserve.

Something to Be Guarded

We need to guard the mind well so it is never taken away from us. If we lose it and then manage to retrieve it, we should still continue to be on guard, for the danger of losing our minds cannot be compared to any other loss of our possessions. Material desires can be tremendous forces of distraction, and can steal our minds. There are five major desires: lust and the desires for food, wealth, fame, and comfort. However, these five desires fan out into an endless array of other desires.

At the center of this thieving family is greed, which commands them all. Behind it reigns the ego, which controls everything. Fighting to preserve our mind against these desires is only possible with the highest level of alertness. It is said that it's extremely difficult, even for ten people, to prevent one thief, if that thief is determined and skillful. Yet, thieves have a body, and luckily, we have security cameras set up these days to capture them. But the thief that steal our mind has no body, so no cameras can capture its movements. It sneaks in and snatches our mind away in a flash, unnoticed.

Within the infinite principles of our mind are infinite treasures, and infinite creative transformations. If we can guard our mind, our bounty will be boundless and inexhaustible, relaxed, and overflowing with riches. This makes the thief even more covetous and unyielding.

To guard against the loss of our mind, we need self-reliance, we need wisdom, and we need *courage*. If these three things are missing, there is no way for us to ward off desires and guard our mind. Indeed, it is even more difficult to reclaim the mind once it has stolen from us. Therefore, it is wiser and simpler to guard it well before this can happen, for then we will not need to make the extra effort to recover it.

The most comfortable and wisest of persons is the one who watches his health when he is healthy, guards his country when it is untroubled, and cultivates his field well when there are no weeds, or when new growth begins to sprout.

If we can guard our mind well in this way, without losing it or allowing it to be taken from us, then we can possess all the things contained in this place of numinous treasure. Blessings never run out no matter how much we use them, producing limitless grace for ourselves and others.

Something to Be Illuminated

Let us shine the light into the realm of our minds. When we find a pitch dark area in our physical world, we turn on a light so we can use the space. Only then can we wisely navigate it and take the steps needed.

The same is true in the realm of our minds. The principle that applies is no different. Just as we need light to shine on dark spaces in our physical world, we need the light of wisdom to shine on the ignorance of our mindscape. In the physical world, a space needs to be illuminated for us to see its layout, structure, and content, and allow us to take steps avoiding danger and ensuring our safety. Once we can see clearly, we can respond appropriately to the given situation, carry out plans, and create grace. The exact same principle applies in the realm of our minds, with even greater urgency.

We need to illuminate the realm of the mind with the lantern of wisdom if we are to see its corners clearly. We can live skillfully in the physical world when our mindscape is illuminated when it responds appropriately to all things we discover in its corners.

When wisdom rises in our mind, it is like the sun rising in the sky. When wisdom sinks in the mind, delusion sets in quickly, like the darkness that falls after the sun sets.

While it is easy to tell when the sun has set, and to take steps to address the darkness of night, we fail to notice when wisdom disappears in our mind. We confuse darkness with daylight and rush about recklessly in our life, only to succumb to trouble—sliding, colliding, and being wounded.

The light of the sun only illuminates the physical world, but the light of wisdom illuminates the metaphysical: great and small, being and nonbeing, right and wrong, gain and loss, retribution and reparation, cause and effect, roots and branches, primary and secondary, and everything from the foundation to the crown—there is nothing the light of wisdom does not shine upon. We need to shine the light of wisdom on the mind.

Yet, the quality of the different kinds of light themselves differ. There is the light of a candle, the light of ten candles, the light of a hundred candles, and light as bright as the sun. Similarly, there is the light of wisdom like a firefly in the darkness, the light of wisdom like a kerosene lamp, the light of wisdom like the flash of dynamite, the light of wisdom like an electric lamp, and the light of wisdom like the sun. Depending on its intensity, we may only manage to illuminate the road right in front of us, or we may shine it on the roads ahead for others, and we may illuminate the road before all the people and living creatures of the world. Without that light, we cannot even find our own way on the road. When the light of wisdom is present, we can manage and take responsibility for the path ahead, for the sake of the entire world and all living creatures in it.

We also see different lights in diverse ways. The blind man may not see even in the glaring light of the sun, while others may be capable of seeing what is around them depending on the light available. All of us have different eyesight capabilities. Some are color blind, some are far-sighted, some are near-sighted. Likewise, we have mental vision in our mind that can see things according to the light that it possesses. This mental vision has several other eyes as well: the wisdom eye, the divine eye, the dharma eye, and the buddha eye. These account for the various spiritual capacities that each of us possesses.

If I were to stop the difficult task of explaining all of this and summarize the main point with an expression that captures everything, I would say that we need to shine the light of wisdom in our mind and possess all of the metaphysical eyes. As a result, we will be able to observe what the light shows, and invariably have no regrets as we live through our eternal life. The mind is something to be illuminated.

Something to Be Straightened

Earlier, I said that our mind has different aspects. Each of us has learned different things over the course of multiple eons and lives. Each of us was born with a different spiritual capacity. And each of us has a different perspective of mind. Just as no two people have the same face, no two people have the same mind. Minds differ from person to person, and they are distorted by suffering arising from the sensory conditions they encounter in the physical world, and, internally, from the torments of Mara's deceptions. This distortion is sometimes severe and sometimes slight. The areas of distortion also differ for each of us. There are areas of severe distortion and areas of minor distortion.

We describe these areas accordingly as strengths and weaknesses. The valley may be deep or shallow, taking on a multitude of shapes and forms. We use the term 'character' to refer to the totality of all these qualities.

So, when a person has a good character, we view him as being a good person. A person with bad character is seen as a bad person, a person with a perfect character is a perfect person, a person with a biased character is a biased person, a person with a grasping character is a grasping person, a person with a humble character is a humble person, a person with an arrogant character is an arrogant person, a person with a rule-abiding character is a rule-abiding person, a person with a rule-breaking character is a rule-breaker, a person with a well-mannered character is a well-mannered person, a person with a rude character is a rude person, and so on and so forth.

However, it goes beyond the character we project into the world. Our character shapes both our future destiny and the destiny of the groups we belong to. As a result, our character flaws create traps in reality that at times can feel like unsurpassable mountains and typhoons.

For this reason, we need to inspect everything present inside our minds to find and realign everything that is amiss. If we do not, we may end up summoning great catastrophe or hardship in the future, and we may send our real-life circumstances reeling into disaster and misfortune. It is like a person driving a car—the slightest bit of distraction can take the lives of many.

Distorted things inside our mind are like undetonated mines. At any moment, there is the possibility of an explosion, dependent upon the right circumstances. This is a profoundly serious problem. We are gravely mistaken to harbor the hope or belief that because we managed to escape once by blind luck, we will continue to remain safe in the future.

While it is impossible to list every instance, we can look at the countless examples of disasters resulting from human error that are reported in the media. In every one of them, the reporter states that the problem was caused by a human mistake. In truth, a flaw in the mind was at play. Of course, we need to address the individual issues, but the truly wise course of action is to find and treat the root cause.

Even though it is evident that the cause-and-effect principles is at play, our commitment to take fundamental steps remains either weak or nonexistent. What has happened?

Straightening out our mind means attending to the most fundamental of all things in this world. It is what is meant by "bringing peace to the world." If we can set our minds right completely, peace will come to the world. Furthermore, we can expect all the disasters that take place due to human error to disappear completely.

Something to Be Tamed

There are things wonderful capabilities in our mind, such as nurturing, care, education, and discipline. When a baby is born, it is like a little animal. At times, it is even less capable and developed than an animal. Humans and animals differ little regarding their instinctive development. Yet, the processes of care, education, discipline, and cultivation take place over the course of our development. This is what is wonderful about human beings—education is a process of training. Our mind becomes trained to an astonishing degree through the process of education and discipline. We can also witness the startling changes that take place in animals when they are trained.

What then would be the result of properly training the mind of the human being, which is such an advanced animal that it has sometimes been called the "supreme creation"? There can be no doubt that the mind harbors ample potential for transformation, depending on how it is trained.

In primitive societies, humans lived animalistic lives determined by their biology. Yet, over many centuries of development, we came to live our lives within today's advanced culture and civilization.

There is no question about this. The question we need to ask ourselves is: how do we train the mind? When our minds are trained, our behavior becomes habit—it becomes our character. If we observe the people in our lives, we see those who are experiencing great hardship because of unhealthy habits acquired in the past such as smoking, drinking, drug addiction, gambling, and so forth. The range of unsound habits is truly vast, including incorrect posture as well as unhealthy diets and lifestyles.

Besides individual errors, we also find examples of mistaken practices by groups. Once irrational and inefficient practices become entrenched, they work against the development of society. Look closely at the underdeveloped countries of the world and you will find that practices without rational or factual basis have become entrenched, sapping important resources from social development.

Among these there are superstitious and irrational practices. For example, in Korea's past, people revered spirits and conducted practices such as selecting auspicious tomb sites or honoring sacred trees. Indeed, there were too many such practices to list them here.

Mind training occurs over the passage of time for both individuals and groups. These trainings may be good or bad, or they may be meaningless. If they are good, they will be beneficial; if they are meaningless or bad, they will be harmful.

Both are the result of mind training. The mind cannot be left unguarded without proper direction. Instead, our mind should be trained to be wise and conform to rules. This training should be done sensibly and efficiently through dharma. A productive mind training requires a basis in dharma instruction, and it needs to culminate in the state of perfect harmony with the essence of our true nature.

If we have properly trained our mind in this way, we can serve as guides with the buddhas and sages. Our every step will transcend the triple world, and everything we do will blossom with the flowering of grace, providing blessings for ourselves and the world. Therefore, our mind is something that should be trained completely and never be neglected.

Something to Be Cultivated

There are a great many things that we human beings need to cultivate while we live in this world. Cultivation of mind is a privilege that is unique to humans. It is difficult to find any examples of cultivation in the animal world. However, cultivation is engrained into human culture.

All the glorious achievements that we see today in the language of art as well as the expressions of sound and design arts are products of cultivation. If we also include the cultivation required in the production of goods, such as farming, then it can truly be said that we humans live lives of cultivation.

There is no corner of our life that is untouched by cultivation. The life of cultivation, extending from our own bodies to our homes, the surrounding environment, and nature, is an inherent human drive. Cosmetics, fashion, design, landscaping are all products of this cultivation. As humans, we at least understand that everything in this world becomes better when it is cultivated, and grows stale or degraded when it is neglected.

Yet, we do not know how to cultivate our own mind. There is scarcely any conscious desire within us to cultivate the mind. As a result, our minds grow twisted and polluted—a detriment that remains invisible to us. Our original mind becomes unproductive and is invaded by all sorts of weeds and brambles, yet we still do not cultivate it. We do not see it, so we do not care. When something is as important as our mind, can we afford not to cultivate it? Of course not. The mind is something that should be cultivated before all else, and with even greater emphasis.

Mind cultivation is at the center of all the other forms of cultivation mentioned above. None of them has any meaning unless we cultivate our minds. Think about it. What point is there in applying beautiful makeup on the outside when the mind inside is uncared for and unwholesome? The same is true for everything else. What is the point of wrapping something foul in precious silk?

We ensure an abundant harvest in the fall when we cultivate our field properly. So it is with our mind. When properly cultivated, it produces endless treasures, great enlightenment, and the boundless ability for creative transformation. What we gain is beyond expression.

Despite this, the reality is that we make little attempt to cultivate our mind. How can this be? Is this a limitation of human beings, the ones who are supposed to be the supreme creatures?

Stranger still is our inability to see the ugliness that results from our failure to cultivate our mind, even though it is clearly apparent to others. If our body is dirty and we smell bad, we do not simply leave it that way; we wipe it off, wash ourselves, change clothes, and we sniff again just to make sure that it has been removed completely. We become very attentive. We react with shame and embarrassment to the odor that reeks from our body.

However, we do not recognize that we should be ashamed and

embarrassed by the ugliness in our minds. Other people sense it, yet we do not. If we can just perceive it, there is hope. So, we cannot simply leave our mind alone. We need to cultivate it thoroughly. How can we ignore or neglect the endlessly wondrous results that we can achieve when we do cultivate it? The mind is something to be cultivated thoroughly.

Something to Be Filled

Our mind is originally empty. "Empty" here means that it is void of content, while "true nature" refers to its essence. Because it is empty, it can admit anything. Indeed, our mind is an endlessly huge vessel that can contain anything and everything in this world. It is a vessel of such size that we cannot see its limits, so its realm is not one that we can understand with our physical concepts of space. No matter how big an object is, once it is filled, it cannot hold anything else. However, in the mind, you can keep putting things into its empty space, and there will always be empty space left over to take in more.

The task is to endlessly fill that empty space and to fill it with what is most necessary. We are gravely mistaken to think of filling it indiscriminately. We do not have the need or the time to clutter our mind with toxic things, instead we should fill our mind with absolutely essential and priceless treasures. Imagine, looking into the warehouse of a person who is disorderly. It becomes hard to tell if it is a garbage dump or a warehouse. It becomes difficult to witness—all that chaos, all the miscellaneous junk.

Now look at the storage space of someone whose affairs are properly in order. Not only will you only see the most essential things, but you will also find that the items are all in their right place.

Anytime something is needed, they can find it, and with the greatest of ease. What kinds of things should we keep in the vast empty space of our mind's storehouse? Should we litter it with garbage, pile it with random things with each passing day? Or should we ensure that it is filled to the brim with priceless treasures? Although we know how to inspect storehouses in our physical reality, we do not know to investigate our mind's storehouse. Even when we do look, we do not know how to make sense of it. The orderly person knows how to size up the mind's storehouse, how to figure out what he to do next and how to respond appropriately. That person organizes the assorted items, and discerns what has value, and what is lacking. This organizational capability allows that person to find and use what is needed at any given moment.

The same applies to the storehouse of our mind. When it is kept amply stocked and orderly, we achieve a life of abundance. When it is understocked, our life is in a state of deprivation. In addition to rare and priceless jewels, the storehouse of a mind like those buddhas and bodhisattvas will contain all the things needed for our household. Plentiful and easily accessible, those items will never run out. With such a storehouse, we can feed every living creature in existence.

In other words, our only task is to clear away the clutter in our mind's storehouse so the inexhaustible goods of supreme enlightenment can be stored there instead.

Our mind's storehouse is where we gather the infinite wisdom, virtue and capabilities that we need to cultivate. As a result, we skillfully manage our home, govern countries, and bring peace into the world.

Something to Be Harnessed

In my earlier explanation of karma, I said that anything can exhibit great power when it binds together. Since karma is formed through the binding together of distracting thoughts, it causes great misfortune for the path ahead of us. What I wish to say here is, when we harness our scattered minds with right energy, it becomes the driving force for producing grace.

There is a principle that states that all things in this world become powerless when they are broken apart—while even the tiniest, most trifling things exhibit a force beyond our imagination when they are brought together. This is true for the spiritual world as well. In psychology, people speak of a "split personality." The condition may sometimes result from problems involving our cranial nerves. Whatever the case, the condition splits our mind apart and leaves it beyond repair, leading inevitably to a breakdown. Once the mind has been split, its weakening becomes unavoidable.

A family is the same way: when it splits apart, all its members are weakened and experience misfortune. Groups and organizations also become weakened when their members are divided. Rifts among the citizens of a country cause that country to weaken and experience misfortune; in severe cases, the country may collapse completely. As a result, many people feel that we are obliged to rally together. However, history has shown us numerous instances of leaders attempting to establish unity while also engaging in improper behavior. Unity is only meaningful when it is based in a just and righteous cause. Otherwise, it leads only to greater misfortune. Leaders and organizations that are wise take steps before a situation can reach this point.

A person or leader who is blind to wisdom will keep going until the situation is beyond repair. In reality, our unity or division creates a force that alters history.

These days, Korean politics are based on a democratic system. Yet too much fixation on any one party can detract from unity among its citizens. It can foster divisions of opinion and disagreements among people, eventually leading the country to ruin. If we are only capable of dividing and show no ability to unite, we will end up collapsing. In our current time, there is an urgent need for unity, but this can only be achieved through logical reasoning and a just cause.

Division consciousness is a situation where one seeks to take sides no matter the cost. Unity consciousness, in contrast, sides with reason and a just and righteous cause. Division is the foundation of ruin, while the power of unity is a driving force for development.

However, unity and division in our physical reality is secondary. Once again, the unity or division of our mind takes precedence. Our physical reality cannot split apart when our mind is united, and our physical reality cannot be united when our mind is divided.

So, the mind is something that must somehow be harnessed. We need to bring together our scattered minds and unite them into one great dynamic mind. The power that will result, will truly be an awesome strength.

If we can harness the original energy of the Dharmakaya Buddha, by which we are linked with the truth of this universe, the power that results is said to be so great that all the malevolent demons and spirits are extinguished of their own accord. This ability to annihilate malevolent demons and spirits is only the beginning: the energy that we harness will give us the strength to achieve whatever we want, to succeed in whatever we do, and to have whatever we need.

When we are filled with the union of benevolent minds, ill-meaning energy and Mara's deceptions dare not come near us. When we are filled with the union of righteous minds, unrighteous energy and Mara's deceptions dare not come near us. When we are filled with the union of well-mannered minds, rude energy and Mara's deceptions dare not come near us. When we are filled with the union of wise minds, foolish energy and Mara's deceptions dare not come near us. When we are filled with the union of faithful minds, disbelieving energy and Mara's deceptions dare not come near us. When we are filled with the union of virtuous minds, heartless energy, and Mara's deceptions dare not come near us. When we are filled with the union of truthful minds, false energy and Mara's deceptions dare not come near us. And when any other good minds are harnessed, wicked and perverse selfishness dare not come near us. We call this, the rightness that wickedness cannot invade.

It is like burning a mosquito coil in our room—the scent fills the air and prevents any mosquitos from coming in. Right energy once harnessed prevents the intrusion of wickedness and perversity.

Not only is wickedness unable to encroach upon us, but positive energy also gives us superpowers. Opening a new world while producing limitless grace. The minds that have been harnessed become the source of all motivating force. When unions are great, great wisdom emerges forth; when they are small, the wisdom is also small. Above all, minds united with the intention of inquiry become crucial sources of awakening.

For this reason, Master Daesan, the Third Head Dharma Master of Won-Buddhism, gave dharma instruction in which he listed the ten right energies to harness. I hope that these provide a useful guideline for the reader's understanding. If the practitioner wishes to perform great practice and achieve great things, he must receive great energy. This energy comes in ten forms:

First, fundamental energy. When we accumulate an abundance of energy by harnessing this great and fundamental energy, all evil spirits and unwholesome thoughts vanish of their own accord.

Second, right energy. When we harness and fill ourselves with right energy that is fair and just, selfishness and perversity will not invade us.

Third, energy of precision and oneness. When we harness and fill ourselves with only energy that is exact and unified, we will consistently maintain our center.

Fourth, vast energy. When we harness and fill ourselves with energy that is vast and unimpeded, a mind that is needy and frustrated will open in an exhilarating way.

Fifth, energy of the dharma. When we harness and fill ourselves with the energy of the right dharma and right way, no delusions will intrude on the path of great power and the great Dharma.

Sixth, middle energy. When we harness and fill ourselves with an energy without bias, without excess or deficiency, our mind will be unwavering, allowing no intrusive thoughts to enter.

Seventh, numinous energy. When we harness and fill ourselves with mystical energy that is ever-bright and ever-numinous, the bedazzlements of perversity and fantasy will not be able to intrude.

Eighth, truth energy. When we harness and fill ourselves with the energy of truth that admits no shred of falsehood, no disguise or exaggeration can intrude.

Ninth, ultimate energy. When we have harnessed and filled ourselves with ultimate energy that courses through the highest heavens, there will be no holes that lead to dissipation.

Tenth, the energy of the great circle. When we have harnessed and filled ourselves with all these energies perfectly and completely, we will possess the great Dharma and great power, achieving only what is perfect and complete.

All of these represent phenomena that result from the energy of many minds unified. The thoughtful person will therefore need to commit him or herself to harnessing their minds.

Something to Be Purified

In the past, teachers in many spiritual traditions made a great deal of effort to purify the minds of human beings. Why did they put so much effort into doing this? Are our minds really so clouded? When we speak of something going from cloudy to clear, we are usually talking about water. Water that has various contaminants mixed into it is said to be polluted, and we speak of purifying the cloudy water that results from this contamination.

Originally, water is clear and unpolluted. Consider water that has been brought up to the surface from deep underground. The water is clean with nothing mixed into it. It is utterly and completely pure. However, once that water has been brought above ground, it is put to many uses or undergoes various processes, pollutants are mixed into it and the water become contaminated and cloudy. Not only does the water lose it inherent vitality, but it comes to possess toxicity. As a result, the water brings harm to the surrounding environment. In severe cases, it becomes a substance that kills. This contamination of water has become an even more severe problem within our industrial society. Once polluted, water must go through a purification process before we can use it. For drinking water in particular, complete purification is essential.

The same principle that applies to water applies to our mind as well. It, too, is purity itself in its original nature, harboring no pollutants of any kind. But as it emerges into the Saha world (mundane world) and engages in various activities, it becomes contaminated with various things. The more contaminated our mind becomes, the murkier it is. The murkier it is, the more severe the contamination, so our original mind loses its vitality and fades into helplessness. Not only that, but the mind also comes to harbor various poisons, creating harm wherever it goes.

Polluted water hurts grass, trees, fish, animals, or the human beings that encounter it. The same is true for the polluted mind. When it enters a family, the polluted mind does damage to the family. When it enters society, the polluted mind damages society. When it enters a country, the polluted mind damages the country. And when it ventures out into the world, the polluted mind does harm to the world. The reach of its harm is too vast to describe in words.

The funny thing is that while people pay a lot of attention to the contamination of water, developing instruments to measure it and inspect it regularly, we pay no attention to the pollution of our minds. The severity of mind pollution has reached a critical level, yet we show no interest in purifying our minds—indeed, we do not even perceive the contamination. And while we work ahead of time to prevent water from being contaminated and to purify it once it has been polluted, we take no steps to plan for or prevent the contamination of our minds. We are simply at a loss.

There has been talk these days about creating a set of standards to measure integrity. However, these standards are results-oriented, and do not address the specific issues concerning the interior of our mind. The damage that results from the failure to tend to our interior mind leaves us experiencing the most intense suffering.

What exactly is it that comes into our mind to pollute it? Just as there are things that contaminate water, there are also things that pollute the mind. There are more of these than we could ever number, but the most toxic, potent, and basic are the three mental poisons of greed, anger, and delusion; the five desires (appetite, lust, material desires, the desire for fame, and the desire for comfort); obsessions; and minds that are attached to misleading ideas. We can expand this list to include all the defilements that cloud our mind. Our mind can never be pure so long as such things are sullying it. And the damages that result are beyond the power of words to express. The need to purify our mind is a task facing the entire world, and it is a crucial matter for all living creatures. Will we purify our minds and make them clear? Or will we simply leave them in their polluted state?

More importantly, the internal state of our mind decides our condition in the outside world. When the mind is clouded, so too is the world of reality. And when the mind is clear, the physical world becomes clear as well. When the mind is in a state of confusion, so is the physical world. And when the mind becomes radiant, the physical world becomes radiant as well.

While people denounce the corruptions of the physical world, we show less interest in the corruptions inside of us. While we busy ourselves with arresting those responsible for corruption and bringing them to court, our efforts to straighten out the minds that are responsible for that corruption are feeble. In such cases, we typically say that a person does not manage his or priorities. In everything we do, there is a principle that states, if you put effort into the fundamentals of anything, the goal will be achieved. How can people disregard this principle when it comes to the mind?

Neither governmental organizations nor common institutions and groups have a department in charge of handling spiritual leadership. They may have an office in charge of "culture," but its duties are confined to the arts. There is no office in charge of the mindscape of the spiritual realm. This is an especially serious flaw in a society dominated by obsession, and we desperately need to address it.

As society has become so very clouded, we have often heard people complain that "those who have power and money go free, while those who don't are found guilty." This is an indication of how severely murky our society is, and it signifies the extensive contamination of our minds.

When our body is severely polluted, we eventually lose our life. A nation or society that is profoundly contaminated is fated to collapse. It may only be revived when we generate a new life that is without pollution. This is a principle of life and a principle of the world.

Therefore, our mind is an object that must be purified. We must purify every corner of our mind, thereby restoring its vitality.

Something to Be Emptied

The true nature of our original mind is void and empty. However, dust and waste are produced as we encounter and struggle with sensory conditions, and they end up strewn all over the space of our mind. We need to remove them and recover the original clean emptiness of our mind.

Our mind is like a film, and physical reality like the object captured on it. Whenever we encounter something, a mind-picture is taken. You can well imagine how cluttered things get as these accumulate. Furthermore, the mind is not senseless. It does not simply leave the captured images in place. The mind is an astonishing thing, one that produces various new worlds out of these images.

Being that our mindscape is incredibly cluttered, we experience terrible pain when we bring all these objects into our mind and try to live with them. It feels as though our head might burst. The modern society that we live in is veritably flooded with the latest products of civilization and culture. Our mind must live with all these things, so you can imagine how cluttered it becomes. This is sending us a strong message: we need emptiness in our mind.

We must clear our mind, empty it again and empty it some more. We must clear away all those various things, sweep them away until nothing more can be cleared out. We need to make it so that any sensory condition that comes to us from our physical reality becomes nothing more than a passing cloud, and not something that occupies a constant place in our mind. The tranquility, the comfort, the leisure we experience when this happens is beyond the power of words to describe. The mind is an object that must be emptied completely.

In addition, we must clear away perverse states of mind when we wish to do what is right. We must clear away petty minds of greed when we make a great vow and set out to achieve it. When we aspire to do something great, we need to clear away the mind that dwells on the small. When we pursue one pointed mind in something, we need to clear away defilements. When we aim to reach the pinnacle stage of any philosophy, we need to clear away all distracting thoughts. With the pinnacle of spiritual practice in particular, true nature will only appear after we have continuously cleared away until there is nothing left.

Therefore, we must empty ourselves of the three poisons of greed, anger, and delusion. We must clear away the mind of the five desires for food, sex, wealth, fame, and comfort. We must clear away the mind of the nine types of sentient beings. We must clear away the mind of the four misleading notions: self (the idea of ego entity), possessiveness (the idea of a person), inferiority (the idea of sentient beings), and superiority (the idea of long life). We must clear away the mind that develops after clearing away the idea of the four misleading notions (the idea of dharma itself). Then we must clear away the mind that develops after we have cleared away the idea of dharma (the idea of non-dharma). Only when we have arrived at the stage where no further clearing away is possible do we become one with the void. We must let go of all minds of fixation on anything. Release, release, release, until there is not a hair's worth of anything left to be released. Only then are great liberation and freedom possible.

Then emptiness becomes added to the void, so that all is equal even when sensory conditions of the real world descend like a thunderstorm—the void remains simply the void. No black clouds that arise can do anything to the void. The void is simply the void and nothing more.

The spiritual mentors of the past described the progress that we achieve in our practice in terms of four stages:

1) **Inscribing in wood.** This is the level where the sensory conditions that come to us are engraved indelibly on our mind. At this stage, we cannot erase the impressions that become implanted there.

2) **Inscribing in mud.** Like writing in wet earth, sensory conditions come and make their mark on the mind, but as time passes, they are gradually resolved or disappear.

3) **Inscribing in water.** There is a brief impression that occurs at the moment we encounter a sensory condition, but it immediately disappears.

4) **Inscribing in air.** Like stamping something into the air, the sensory conditions that arrive have never come. Those that go, have never gone. Those that are present are absent, and those that are absent are absent. This is the pinnacle stage.

The realm of inscribing in air is called the realm of samadhi and the hall of silent illumination, the source of the light of wisdom, the original source of all things, the realm that transcends being and non-being, the unequaled realm, and the realm that cannot be matched by the myriad dharmas.

It is a realm devoid of the five aggregates (form, sensation, perception, will, and consciousness), the eighteen realms (the six sense organs, six types of sensory conditions, and six consciousnesses), and the four noble truths (suffering, the origin of suffering, the cessation of suffering, and the path leading to the cessation of suffering), the twelve causes (ignorance, formations, consciousness, name and form, the six sense gates, contact, sensation, desire, attachment, becoming, birth, and aging/death), containing nothing that is thought to be understood through awakening, nor anything that is thought to be comprehended. All is simply resting. The only thing that remains is the purity of drinking water when thirsty, eating when hungry, and sleeping when weary.

In this way, we enter the realm of the great samadhi, the realm without action or rest, the realm of simultaneous action and rest and is thus united with the Dharma and principles of the *Heart Sutra*.

This realm is one in which all comparing minds have ceased and all quarrelling has ended. We call this "samadhi without conflict."

Let us examine these comparing minds a bit more closely.

When our comparing mind becomes enhanced, we tend to pick a side. If we do not stop doing this, we end up divided, and division leads us into the path of collapse. Thinking they are undertaking great work, the foolish person lives and dies taking sides. Not only does he do endless harm to his organization, his group or community, but he creates endless transgressive karma for himself.

But the wise person who has entered samadhi without conflict busies himself with quieting the storms of the multitude of quarrels, dissolving them, and embracing them, fusing them into a single whole. Internally, he is devoted to unity through realizing the true self; externally, he is devoted to unity through realizing the great self.

So, with its inexhaustible radiance and great capacity and functioning, there is no object that the enlightened mind does not embrace in its mysterious principles, nor any living creature that exists outside its merciful shade.

As this indicates, our mind is an object that must be emptied completely. This is an urgent task that is of paramount importance for practitioners of the Dharma.

CHAPTER 5

PRACTICE TO CULTIVATE THE MIND

Spiritual Practice

I have given a general description of how our mind works. What I have described so far is not everything there is to know about the principles of the mind. I have merely touched on the most general aspects. These mind-worlds are said to be so endlessly vast and numerous that there is nothing that lies outside them. At the same time, they can be so small and few that discerning them is almost impossible.

It is impossible to explain everything that is encompassed by the mind. Indeed, we could use everything in this world, and it would not be enough.

However, we do not need to drink the Pacific Ocean to know the taste of its water. One sip from anywhere in the sea will and we will experience its full flavor.

Comprehension of the mind is not the issue. The core question is, "What should we do with this mind?" Only when this question stands out in great relief and is grasped so firmly that we cannot let go, have we even begun to approach its truth. This allows us the possibility of eventually finding the answer and powerfully bringing it forth.

Let us begin our search for the answer to this question.

The answer is provided almost perfectly for us in the scriptures of

Won-Buddhism. Through this introduction and explanation, we will attempt to find a definitive answer.

I recognize the mind-set that immediately rejects certain religions. If the religion offers a clear way, should we simply reject it blindly and continue living with our suffering?

Won-Buddhism has presented, taught, and encouraged the understanding of the spiritual teachings of all the religions in the past with utmost clarity.

All those who refer to and practice them will reap benefits and eventually attain great enlightenment.

In our practice, we must comprehend the principle of the mind and engage our efforts to conform to it. With the repetition of these personal efforts, this principle of mind will be established as our true character. No matter how much we may have comprehended the principle, if we do not follow this up with personal practice, it is like a tree with a good trunk, good branches, and good flowers that bears no fruit.

As we practice, we need to gather our own power and draw on the assistance of others. Our mastery grows more effectively when we find a teacher and cultivate the Way with fellow practitioners. As all of us experience this together—teacher, student, and colleagues—it becomes both a collective and individual discipline. The rough edges get polished down, the empty spaces are filled, and our discipline of our true nature rapidly becomes more and more balanced.

When we practice with others, we experience moments of awakening and inner transformation. We can utilize the experiences and awakenings of others and continuously replenish our vow so that our determination to practice becomes stronger. We need to make a concentrated effort to strengthen our mind and invigorate our faith. This effort is profoundly enhanced when we practice in community.

Let us start, then, on the path of practice to cultivate the mind.

Reason and Practice

We must first consider the question of rationality.

Rationality describes reasonable behaviors that conform to principle, whereas irrationality refers to unreasonable behaviors that violate principle. The unreasonable will never bring success, no matter how hard we work, while the reasonable will allow us to succeed in the efforts we make. Wisdom is our ability to pursue rationality.

In simpler terms, it is rational to make a bowl of rice by boiling grains of rice; it is irrational to make rice by boiling sand. It is rational to make a mirror out of glass and irrational to make one by polishing a roof tile.

Nothing in this world succeeds when we use irrational methods. Effort only pays off when combined with least a tiny sliver of rationality!

Our practice is no exception to this rule. It must be utterly rational, reasonable, and based on truth. Practice that is not based on the principle of truth will produce hollow results or none at all. There is a danger that, even if we practice a lot, we risk developing a bias in our character.

Practice returns us to the original source of our true nature and our original mind. Our true nature is the core of spiritual vitality and has limitless force. Practice is the process of finding spiritual vitality and acquiring the limitless power of the truth.

This does not mean that we should engage in vague asceticism, forbearance practice, or exertion practice. Teachers of the past used expressions such as "like trying to polish a tile into a mirror" or "like crushing grass with a stone" to warn against irrational methods.

Our practice must align with the principle of the truth. While the truth has characteristics of limitless diversity, it can be separated into two main strands: substance and function. Substance is often described as "true voidness," an emptiness of all things, while function can be described as "marvelous existence," or the presence of everything that is manifested in a marvelous way.

These are two main directions in our practice: emptying our mind completely (Substance) and the presence of everything that is manifested in a marvelous way (Function).

When these two core elements are missing from our practice, we can easily find ourselves fighting doggedly for the wrong thing, which ultimately ends in wasted time and wasted mental and spiritual energy.

If I were to capture this spirit of using our six sense organs, it would be this: manifest and use them in a complete and perfect way, one that is utterly impartial and selfless.

Completeness and perfection, utter impartiality and selflessness—these must be our practice standards while using our six sense organs: our eyes, ears, nose, mouth, body, and mind. Even if the practitioner engages in a special kind of practice and has unique capabilities, he is on the wrong path of practice if his command of the true nature and actions of his six sense organs fall short of completeness and perfection, utter impartiality, and selflessness. We must guard against this.

Now, this is not the original intention of practice. With our practice, we must be able to preserve perfection in body and mind, achieve perfect understanding of human affairs and universal principles, and make perfect use of our body and mind. This is where the true meaning of practice lies. When we achieve this, we gain the ability to enter a world of mastery, liberation, and freedom. We will freely come and go among the three realms of existence and the six destinies without impediments in our affairs or obstructions to our principles. In our practice, we must constantly examine whether we are using our body and mind completely and perfectly, utterly impartially and selflessly.

In order to achieve this perfection, we must accumulate the powers of Spiritual Cultivation, Cultivation of Wisdom and Inquiry, and Choice in Action.

This sometimes confuses practitioners who have strayed from this principle and the right dharma and Way. Someone may experience a light that arises like a firefly in the darkness as the result of strenuous practice and may mistakenly believe that he or she has somehow reached a special stage. Or perhaps he or she has been visited by a spirit and predicted the future. That practitioner may dwell on such an experience and become blinded by it, as though it were spiritual communion. We often see cases like this. These are all temporary phenomena found among people of weak spiritual ability and may lure them into great transgressions and evil. We are at risk when we fail to control our own spirit and become deeply entangled in phenomena.

Spiritual possession is the state of being occupied by an object that exploits the weakness of our subject. Since these stem from weaknesses in the subjective spirit, they are a far cry from the kind of practice that is based on a fearsome spiritual ability. Indeed, they obstruct our path. Should such supernatural powers occur before we have brought the three mental poisons and five desires into submission internally, they will be used to satisfy our own desires. As a result, we may commit terrible transgressions.

There is one more thing that may cast a spell on us.

Prophecies and mind-reading occurred frequently in the past. These also result from mistaken practice when those who encounter these phenomena have not mastered and understood the principles of great and small, being and nonbeing, and of the retribution and response of cause and effect. In other words, they occur because of problems of spiritual health. With every phenomenon that takes place in this world, there is movement of energy that takes place before they appear or some energy that paves the way for them beforehand. Before the rain comes, rain energy comes. The actual rain that falls is simply the final expression. In Korea, there is something called "bad weather behavior," or the strange things that people do when the weather is poor. People with poor nerves do strange things even when the weather is perfectly fine. They are simply experiencing the rain energy before the rain comes. People with healthy nerves are not affected by the weather; they are not subject to the influences of the wind and the cold, the heat and humidity. These are people in good health. The weaker our spiritual health, the more sensitive we are to new energies, and this "bad weather behavior" is the phenomenon that results.

This is a trap that practitioners are prone to fall into. We must be wary of it, and those who encounter it should also avoid becoming deluded.

We simply need to have the sprouting and growing, blooming and fruition of the rational right dharma and Way in our practice. We should follow along the right path that is set out for us.

The Possibilities of Mind Practice

Mind Practice or Spiritual Cultivation—what does this mean? The dictionary gives several definitions, so I think it best to use the word *mastery*.

For human beings, survival is a matter of using all the resources we have in this world. We cannot live or survive without them. These resources may be temporal or spatial in nature, and they come from many objects we see. Before we use any of these objects, we must go through a process of mastering their use. Once complete mastery is achieved, these resources will benefit ourselves and all others. However, without mastery these resources can bring disaster on us and others. Mastery is essential.

One of the modern conveniences we all enjoy these days is the car. We cannot deny the tremendous difference a car makes.

We cannot take advantage of the car and all the benefits it affords without first mastering how to drive it. We need to master driving the car and train ourselves to drive carefully. We must master the skill of driving before we can drive with peace of mind and use the car freely to make our life easier and more abundant.

Certainly, this is not just true for the car. Nothing in the world exists outside this principle. It is crucial for us to master the things in our life. There is simply no comparison between a life of mastery and a life without it.

Of all the areas that require *mastery*, the most fundamental is *the mind*. There is never a time when we stop using our mind. It is used whenever we experience anything, internally or externally. So, the mind truly does sit at the center of our experience.

It is very risky to use the mind without achieving mastery of it. It is like taking the wheel of a car without ever having practiced driving.

The principle of disciplining our mind is even more complicated and marvelous than the workings of the most sophisticated vehicle.

This principle, as complex, strange, and marvelous as it is, demands more complete knowledge and mastery. When something is used at a fundamental level, its comprehension is a matter of the highest priority. Such is the case with mind practice and cultivation of the mind.

The mind contains limitless possibility. It lacks form, making it extremely difficult to grasp. But it clearly exists; there is nothing that is not connected to it, nothing that it does not know, nothing that it cannot do, and nothing that it does not do. All things are created by the mind.

The mind can shatter bliss into pieces and create hell. It can shatter hell into pieces and create bliss. It creates fortune and misfortune, calamity and happiness, rising and falling, prosperity and decline. The mind guides all human history and everything that happens in nature.

Will we master the art of the mind? Or will we abandon it and deal with the world impetuously?

This is the meaning of mind practice and cultivation:

With cultivation, there is progression and grace.
Without cultivation, there is only regression and harm.

The Mind and Sensory Conditions

First, we need to understand what is meant by sensory conditions.

Sensory conditions have nothing to do with us, functioning only according to their own properties. When our mind encounters them, we respond in various ways. These responses create emotions of joy, anger, sadness, and pleasure. Our responses generate fortune and misfortune. Sensory conditions exist independent from us, independent from our mind and possessing their own unique characteristics. Those conditions ultimately become the resources used by our mind.

Sensory conditions relate to our six senses (sight, hearing, smell, taste, touch, and will) and the various external conditions, favorable or adverse.

In addition to serving as resources for our mind, sensory conditions may seem to try to swallow us whole. In other words, the six sensory conditions represent six gateways through which Mara's minions invade and try to occupy us. The three conditions represent three channels through which these minions pass. They are similar, in a sense, to the land, sea, and air routes in national defense.

We can easily think of examples such as lust, wealth, honor, sleep and idleness, and the list goes on and on.

When we overcome any kind of sensory condition, it can be used as a resource and become our ally. But when we are overwhelmed by it, it will dominate our mind, enslaving us under the minions of Mara.

Good use of sensory conditions results in grace and leads us to wisdom and the development of strength and perseverance. Bad use results in harm and leads us to greed, anger, delusion, and finally to resignation and abandonment.

The practicing mind takes every sensory condition as material for practice. Every moment becomes an opportunity for practice. Sensory conditions provide us with a training ground and an inexhaustible storehouse of content.

Those who handle sensory conditions capably transform raging typhoons into gentle breezes. Those who lack the ability to handle sensory conditions well, transform even the gentle breeze into a typhoon. They can easily be overwhelmed by the mildest of circumstances.

In short, it is a matter of training the mind. However, we should be mindful of something that has happened repeatedly throughout history and continues to happen today. Practitioners often abandon the duties and obligations of their secular lives because they consider them to be obstacles to attaining the Way. As a result, they retreat deep into the mountains and valleys to avoid their duties. While it may be beneficial to avoid sensory conditions for a while and recharge ourselves, especially after a period of strenuous practice, we need to understand that these sensory conditions or difficult situations are material for our practice. If we maintain the view that all sensory conditions are an impediment to practice, our practice will fail.

The steadfast practitioner tackles sensory conditions directly and overcomes them. The practitioner should understand the need to train amid sensory conditions and challenging situations.

Cultivation develops discipline in the details of our daily lives. There are two types of discipline: cultivation of mind and cultivation of temperament. We will only succeed in developing both types of cultivation when we practice amid sensory conditions. Sensory conditions are like the water when we are learning to swim or the road when we are learning to drive. One cannot learn to swim without being in the water or learn to drive without taking the car on the road.

There is an old saying: "Wisdom never grows without experience." We have experienced how much wisdom is obtained when encountering the sensory conditions of reality.

I remember reading the memoirs of a businessman who had a successful career in Japan. This person had suffered great misfortune as a child: losing his parents at a young age, dropping out of elementary school, and suffering from very poor health. Nonetheless, this served as the force that turned his life into a success. He had to become wise to the world early because he had lost his parents. He studied his whole life due to his feelings of inadequacy. He was always attentive to his health because it had been very poor in the past. This, he said, was how he became successful.

This is how sensory conditions can be used. They are resources which allow us to learn even from tragedy.

It is all a question of the mind. The practitioner's task is to ask how to view sensory conditions, how to respond to them, and how to control them.

Through ongoing encounters with sensory conditions, the

practitioner gains the experience necessary to practice. We should be grateful for sensory conditions and recognize that they contain the light of hope for the future.

The Resources for Mind Practice

There are certain essential resources required for cultivation of the Way. Externally, we have sensory conditions and time; internally, we have the body and the mind. I adopted two phrases from the scriptures as a motto for my life: "Every sensory condition is material for practice, every moment an opportunity to practice."

The true practitioner makes use of every sensory condition as a means for more effective practice, allowing none to pass by unused. Every time sensory conditions present us with practice, we must use the opportunity, rather than look for something else. This is the real material for practice. We must adjust our thinking accordingly.

The same is true for time. Every new moment comes to us, presenting a unique opportunity for practice. Time never returns. If we miss it, we lose it forever. We human beings live under the mistaken belief that since years and days go through a regular cycle, the time that passes us by will visit us again. The spring, summer, fall, and winter that will come in the future are not the same ones that passed by before; they are entirely new seasons. This day and this night are not the same day and night as yesterday. This is also true for each passing moment.

We would be mistaken to think that we can forget about this

moment and practice at some other moment. In doing so, we are missing a golden opportunity. When we let that chance go, we lose it forever. We should understand that time is irreplaceably precious.

Many things can be regained, should we lose them. Time cannot. Time is invaluable because we can never retrieve it once it passes.

For this reason, I hold these words in my mind: "Every sensory condition is material for practice, every moment a chance for practice." These are the very words that I have used to awaken myself.

We need to appreciate the value of time and the awareness of our sensory conditions. We waste our time, our mental energy, and our financial resources by looking at things that do not need to be looked at. We waste our time, our mental energy, and our financial resources listening to things that do not need to be listened to. We waste our time, our spiritual energy, and our financial resources doing things that are not important. We waste our time doing nothing. We waste years of our life in quarreling needlessly with others. When we argue over the weeds that grow in other people's fields, we fail to notice the weeds growing in our own.

The person who respects time as a valuable resource and uses each moment as an opportunity for growth will be fulfilled by everything he does.

So far, I have given a general explanation of time and sensory conditions. These are the external resources for our practice. Now, I will turn to the mind and body. They constitute the internal resources for mind practice.

As I explained before, the mind is the original mover—nothing happens without the mind arising. It was once said that "there is no buddha outside the mind, no dharma outside our true nature." The mind is the buddha, and our true nature is the dharma, so our nature and our mind together are the foundation for practitioners to attain buddhahood.

The way we manage our thoughts is extremely importance. It does not make sense to Cultivate the Way, while embracing distracting thoughts. Managing our wandering and delusive thoughts form the heart of our practice. It is what makes practitioners sacred.

We must assess every thought that emerges. Is it a right thought or an idle, meaningless one? Right thoughts come together one by one to form a philosophy. Philosophies come together to form character. A sacred character creates sages, buddhas, and bodhisattvas.

Thus, our mind constitutes the primary resource for our practice and cultivation of the Way. We must take great care to cultivate the mind.

The next resource is the body. Along with the mind, the body is a primary internal resource for our practice. Not only is it inseparable from the mind, but it is the mover that produces actions directly from the mind.

The physical body has a peculiar instinct; it is forever trying to chase sensory experiences, despite our mind's will and intention. The physical body can be childish. Like a wayward calf, it prances this way and that, unaware that it may end up trampling the grain in someone's field. Our physical body can generate great consternation.

Yet the mind can do nothing without the physical body. We cannot do anything with our mind alone. The mind can only function through the body and therefore, must handle the body wisely and well.

Conversely, without our body, we could never attain buddhahood. Our body is our vehicle to exert ourselves, accumulate merits, and do great. The mind has the capacity to do anything through this body, including carrying out great ideas.

Another old saying tells us "Overcome the body and follow custom." We cannot do anything unless we overcome the immaturity of the physical body. Our body will be a loyal subject once we have conquered it, but if we have failed to do so it will fall prey to temptation after temptation. The way in which our mind exerts its will over our body determines our journey to buddhahood.

So, the body is something that must be present with the mind during the process of attaining buddhahood, and it is a primary resource for our mind practice. It is a wonderful gift that we have been granted as these invaluable resources can maximize the effectiveness of our mind practice and the efficiency of our cultivation.

As long as time and sensory conditions exist externally and the mind and body exist internally, we can accomplish anything and everything.

The Scriptures and Dharma Instructions

Scripture study is indispensable, for every practitioner. They are key texts written by all the scholars of the Way reaching back into the past and all the way to the present day. They represent a treasure trove of truth and loving-kindness.

The writings we call "scripture" are filled with words of salvation out of the sea of suffering, words for rescue from darkness, words that elucidate the truth, words that guide us on the path of practice, and words of the embodiment of loving-kindness. We must create the foundation of our practice and gauge its progress by the standards set in the dharma instructions contained in the scriptures and taught by all spiritual mentors. These are rules we should take as our overarching guide, the path we must walk. They are also the light that brightly illuminates our path. These dharma words are an inexhaustible storehouse and treasure. They are medicine and treatment to deliver sentient beings and cure the world. They are the path to follow to achieve anything and a vessel filled with the will of great loving-kindness and compassion that rescues us from the sea of suffering. These teachings will melt away the ice of our karmic obstacles. These questions provide the key to awakening. If we study each of these questions, we gain the awakening of understanding. We arrive at the stage of all-penetrating knowledge.

The practitioner must therefore live his life with the scriptures. He must not let go of them for even a moment. While there may be stages of communication of the dharma without words and of accessing the human mind directly, even these must be sought within the teachings of the scriptures.

There is a Chinese saying: Before a saint is born, the way is in the Heavens (the realm of universal truth). When the saint comes to the world, the way resides with the saint. When the saint passes away, the way is in the scripture. This means that practitioners should seek the truth within the heavens, earth, and nature before the sage is born. After a sage is born, practitioners need to seek the truth from the living sage. When the sage passes away, practitioners should rely on scripture to learn the truth.

If there is one jewel that is more priceless than anything in this world, it is the dharma teaching. Its benefits can manifest endlessly. For this reason, the merits of dharma instruction are said to exceed even those of charity, bestowing enough of the seven treasures to fill the world. Such is the power of dharma instruction.

The dharma instructions contained in the scriptures are truly the most precious of jewels. This is why they are called "dharma jewels." The characteristics of the scriptures may vary. Each of them presents a different path or uses different expressions. Some may be greater or lesser, but all of them represent a light, a path, and loving-kindness bestowed upon sentient beings in accordance with our spiritual capacity.

When we are told to "honor the teachings of sages and to accept them respectfully" or to "believe, receive, honor, and execute them," these words are intended to awaken our consciousness to the dharma instructions and make us aware of how humbly we should receive them.

The scriptures truly are a textbook for the practitioner. When practitioners neglect the scriptures, it is like a student who neglects his textbook or study guide. How can they expect their practice to advance?

The person who understands the value of the dharma instructions chooses to embrace them at all times. The scriptures are a veritable storehouse of such instructions. We must keep these scriptures near to us, so that we may read and recite them. Thus, we will naturally immerse ourselves in the truth of these instructions. It has been said that when you read something three hundred times, the meaning is absorbed naturally. This means that when we read and re-read the teachings of the scriptures and we act in accordance with them. We feel the essence of the scriptures and in turn the scriptures fill our nature. Finally, there is nothing in the universe that is not reflected in the scriptures.

Since each person has a different spiritual capacity, there are many possible paths of practice. We have no way of knowing which road will lead us to that crucial moment of connection. When we encounter the right dharma instruction for our spiritual capacity, and that flash of light goes off in our mind, then everything will be resolved in its turn. We can reach the stage where we have no constraints in universal principles or human affairs. That is practice.

None of this is possible unless we honor and practice the dharma instructions as something of utmost value. The practitioner should therefore always keep the scriptures of the past and present close at hand.

Of course, we cannot expect to succeed, if we dwell solely on the words while neglecting to seek out and practice their meaning. We must also focus our efforts on discovering the true nature of the content beyond the words of the scriptures. In doing so, we may enter the right path without wandering down the wrong one.

Threefold Practice
: The Three Elements of The Mind's Life

All things in this world are made up of constituent parts that form the foundation of existence. For example, the three main nutrients that make up our bodies are proteins, carbohydrates, and fat. The three major components of plant fertilizer are nitrogen, phosphoric acid, and calcium. The three prerequisites for Humans are clothing, food, and shelter, while a country requires citizens, territory, and sovereignty.

Similarly, there are three principles that constitute our mind practice. We call them the Threefold Practice of meditation (samadhi), wisdom (prajna), and precepts (sila). In Won-Buddhism, we speak of the Threefold Practice (Spiritual Cultivation, Cultivation of Wisdom and Inquiry, and Choice in Action) as well as the three great powers of the mind (the Power of Spiritual Cultivation, the Power of Wisdom and Inquiry, and the Power of Choice in Action). Buddhism and Won-Buddhism may express concepts differently, but they both present standards for the life of practice.

The three great strengths of the mind that arise from The Threefold Practice make up the three pillars that support our mind, the three great principles of mind practice, and the three great directions for opening an unlimited future. They represent the key to solving the problems of our minds. Any problem that we face can be resolved through the Threefold Practice.

Various spiritual cultivation groups have arisen in recent years to provide guidance in different methods of practice, but they rarely proceed outside the Threefold Practice. The power of the Threefold Practice and the three great powers of the mind lie in the way that these methods of practice are combined. This is difficult for people to understand. Therefore, a more detailed explanation is in order.

The Threefold Practice consists of Spiritual Cultivation, Cultivation of Wisdom and Inquiry, and Choice in Action. To put it in more familiar terms, they guide us to make choices based on sound thought. These are the three major prerequisites for our spiritual life.

Humans accomplish very little when they do not utilize these three spiritual efforts. Even thieves, in the act of stealing, draw upon an equation of sound + thought + choice. This equation is employed in all situations, large or small. When the Threefold Practice is used properly and thoroughly, we can realize anything and everything to perfection.

Our goal is to develop the three great strengths of the mind through the discipline of Threefold Practice. Once we have developed them sufficiently, there will be nothing in this world that we cannot handle. Even, freedom from birth and death, and liberation from the cycle of rebirths become possible for us.

In fact, we all live our spiritual lives according to the Threefold Practice, whether we are aware of it or not. We may have never heard the term "Threefold Practice," but we employ them when we face a problem. We *concentrate* our mind on it. Then, we *inquire* into how to resolve it. Finally, we *determine* what we will do. This is the essence of the Threefold Practice. In much the same way that we breath without awareness of the air, we may not be aware of employing the Threefold Practice even we are doing so all the time. Just as we cannot live physically without clothing, food, and shelter; we cannot live spiritually without Spiritual Cultivation, Cultivation of Wisdom and Inquiry, and Choice in Action.

This is also true for animals. Notice how the cat chooses its actions when a mouse is in front of it. First, it focuses its attention. Then it plots to seize the crucial moment. And finally, it takes action and pounces. This is the Threefold Practice. Every sentient creature uses it in its life. The Threefold Practice represents the three main elements and three main supports that sustain the mind's existence and are the prerequisites of our spiritual life and development.

Each of us differs in our awareness of this principle. There is a world of difference between developing our capabilities with the three great powers of the mind and simply doing without such capabilities.

The Threefold Practice therefore represents the three main elements and prerequisites of spiritual life.

The Threefold Practice could also be said to represent "three great veins of ore" where we may locate our spiritual treasures. As we dig deeper, we find countless precious jewels. The three veins of Spiritual Cultivation, Cultivation of Wisdom and inquiry, and Choice in Action represent a place where a limitless bounty of treasure waits.

Master Chongsan, the Second Head Dharma Master of Won-Buddhism, summarized the principles of the Threefold Practice through a dharma instruction.

Spiritual Cultivation requires two tasks.

One involves purifying; the other involves nourishing.

The junk that litters our mind must be cleared away and our true nature must be nourished, so that it thrives.

The two tasks we face when addressing human affairs and universal principles are to further illuminate them by cultivating wisdom to thoroughly investigate their origins.

The Cultivation of Wisdom and Inquiry has two tasks. One is to cultivate our wisdom as a mirror during daily activities and the other is to thoroughly investigate the root source of all things.

There are also two tasks that we engage in to accumulate good karma and clear away bad karma created by our actions. This means to acquire the correct way, while abandoning anything that is incorrect.

The two tasks of Choice in Action are to accumulate good karma and clear bad karma as we use our six sense organs.

We must also utilize specific methods for carrying out the Threefold Practice:

For Spiritual Cultivation, we must take advantage of every opportunity to develop one pointed mind through reciting the buddha's name and practicing sitting meditation. We should blend practice with the precepts and wisdom as we dedicate our one-pointed mind to each and everything we do in life through Timeless and Placeless Meditation

For Cultivation of Wisdom and Inquiry, we should improve our knowledge by broadening our experience daily, study the dharma to master the methods of practice, and enlist the aid of practice with meditation and the precepts as we use our thoughts to investigate human affairs and universal principles.

For Choice in Action, we must gather large amounts of experience in our daily life, focus mindfully on everything we do, and reduce error to ensure seamless action at crucial moments. We need the help of meditation and wisdom to develop the ability to choose the right and abandon the wrong action.

There are ways for us to measure our progress with the three great powers of the mind and see where we stand in our practice with the Threefold Practice.

To measure our **Power of Spiritual Cultivation**:

We observe in times of rest how often our minds are disturbed. If it happens frequently, our power of Spiritual Cultivation is insufficient. The less often our minds are disturbed, the greater our power of Cultivation is becoming.

We also observe in times of action to see whether we are drawn by the five desires of hunger, lust, material greed, the desire for honors, and the desire for ease, or by the things that we typically enjoy. If we are often attracted by these things, our power is lacking. The less often and intensely we are drawn, the greater our power of Cultivation is becoming.

To measure our **Power of Cultivation of Wisdom and Inquiry**:

We look inside for any obstructions to understanding of the scriptures or understanding our original mind and its true nature. As the obstructions reduce, we can see that our power of Wisdom and Inquiry is improving.

We look outside of ourselves to see if our judgement of objects is accurate. If we are accurately discerning of the objects we encounter, then our power of Wisdom and Inquiry has improved.

To measure our **Power of Choice in Action**:

We observe internally by looking at our mind diary and to what extent we observe the precepts or mindfulness items. If either of these is lacking, our power of Choice in Action is insufficient, but if both are certain and advanced, then our power of Choice in Action is developing.

We observe externally by examining whether our abilities are consistently up to the demands of every occasion. If they are not, this means that our power is lacking; if they are, this means that our power of Choice in Action has developed.

If we practice intently and consistently with the Threefold Practice, we will eventually begin to see results.

The result of Spiritual Cultivation is the power to use the mind freely. We can attain freedom from birth and death, perfect bliss, and success in everything we do.

The result of Cultivation of Wisdom and Inquiry is brighter and clear wisdom of the mind. We can master human affairs and universal principles, endlessly produce the dharma to deliver all sentient beings, and succeed in whatever we do.

The result of Choice in Action is the emergence of practical abilities, allowing us to attain perfect blessings and success in whatever we do through numerous virtuous acts.

Accumulation of the Three Great Powers at Rest: We accumulate the three great powers through retreat practice and through disciplining ourselves when we are not engaged in daily activities. Our spiritual cultivation practice consists of reciting the buddha's name and practicing sitting meditation. Our practice to cultivate wisdom and Inquiry involves studying scriptures, studying the universal principles, and working with koans. Our practice with Choice in Action consists of keeping a mindfulness diary, monitoring whether we are abiding by the precepts well, and minimizing our transgressions or misdeeds.

Application of the Three Great Powers in Action: We apply the three great powers by disciplining ourselves when we are involved in daily activities and through consistent mind training. Spiritual Cultivation practice consists of bringing our mind to a pause to restore our true nature which is already sound and whole whenever we encounter difficult situations.

Nine Paths for Daily Spiritual Cultivation

1. The mind is originally free from disturbance, but disturbances arise in response to sensory conditions; let us restore the equanimity of our true nature by letting go of disturbances.
2. The mind is originally free from delusion, but delusions arise in response to sensory conditions; let us restore the wisdom of our true nature by letting go of delusions.
3. The mind is originally free from wrong-doing, but wrong-doings arise in response to sensory conditions; let us restore the precepts of our true nature by letting go of wrong-doings.
4. Let us replace disbelief, greed, laziness, and ignorance with belief, zeal, questioning, and dedication.
5. Let us turn a life of resentment into a life of gratitude.
6. Let us turn a life of dependency into a life of self-reliance.
7. Let us turn reluctance to learn into willingness to learn well.
8. Let us turn reluctance to teach into willingness to teach well.
9. Let us turn lack of public spirit into eagerness for the public's welfare.

The Essential Dharmas of Daily Practice present us with all the basic principles that we need to study and practice. By principles, we are referring to an index of the core tenets that encompass all dharmas.

The doctrine of Won-Buddhism centers on the circle (O), which symbolizes the truth. It establishes two gateways: the **Gateway of Faith** and the **Gateway of Practice**. The Gateway of Faith includes the **Essential Way of Human Life** with the Fourfold Grace (the Grace of Heaven and Earth, the Grace of Parents, the Grace of Fellow Beings, and the Grace of Laws) and the Four Essentials (developing self-power, the primacy of the wise, educating others' children, and venerating the public-spirited). The Gateway of Practice includes the **Essential Way of Practice** with the Threefold Practice (Spiritual Cultivation, Cultivation of Wisdom and Inquiry, and Choice in Action) and the Eight Articles (the Four Articles to Develop—belief, zeal, questioning, and dedication, and the Four Articles to forsake—disbelief, greed, laziness, and ignorance).

The Fourfold Grace and Four Essentials (representing the Essential Way of Human Life) and the Threefold Practice and Eight Articles (representing the Essential Way of Practice) are included as areas for everyday practice among these Nine Essential Dharmas. The Threefold Practice is included in Items 1, 2, and 3; the Eight Articles in Item 4; the Fourfold Grace in Item 5; and the Four Essentials in Items 6, 7, 8, and 9.

These Essential Dharmas of Daily Practice represent the totality of the Won-Buddhist teaching. Nevertheless, they are not exclusively required by Won-Buddhism. They are essential terms and principles for anyone who wishes to live the most rational and efficient lives throughout eternity. They are marvelous methods that can influence all areas of our life. I will hold off for now on explaining the Nine

Essential Dharmas of Daily Practice and focus first on examining what they signify.

We are instructed to put these Nine Essential Dharmas into everyday practice, monitoring and examining them constantly. If we commit them to memory and practice them repeatedly, it is said, this will be sufficient for us to attain buddhahood. We are told to examine them periodically and to examine them every day and every month. But what should we be looking for?

Reflections for Everyday Practice

Did I experience disturbance in my mind today? (The capacity of the great virtuous one)

Did I experience delusion in my mind today? (The wisdom of the great virtuous one)

Did I experience wrong-doing in my mind today? (The virtue of the great virtuous one)

Did I pursue belief, zeal, questioning, and dedication? (The motivating force for success in all things)

Did I live my life filled with gratitude today? (The harmonious aspect of deep appreciation for life)

Did I live a life of self-reliance today? (Autonomy)

Did I learn with a sincere mind today? (Wise person)

Did I teach with a sincere mind today? (Instructor)

Did I bring benefit to others today? (Helping others)

These words are so plain, we may be inclined to take them lightly, to dismiss them as simple and superficial. For this reason, we ought to examine the Nine Essential Dharmas in greater depth.

As indicated in the dharma instruction above, the first, second, and third articles describe the capacity, wisdom, and virtue of the great virtuous one. The fourth illuminates the motivating force for success in all things, while the fifth identifies the great power of life appreciation. We gain complete power of autonomy through the sixth and can become a wise person with the seventh. The eighth allows us to become a leader, and the ninth leads us to become a great administrator.

When we examine all these closely, we see that these Nine Essential Dharmas that fully open the great road for Mahayana practice. The essential intention of the way of Mahayana practice allows us to practice with one another under any circumstances and to deliver a living creature from any situation. Its method of practice that enables us to deliver all sentient beings.

Let us examine the proof.

These Nine Essential Dharmas of Daily Practice outline a wonderful methodology that we can use in any situation we may encounter. Since they encompass both the Essential Way of Practice and the Essential Way of Human Life, they help us to discipline ourselves through their practice and they allow us to firmly establish the fundamentals of the framework for the buddha. This is the road to our own enlightenment and the enlightenment of others. The Nine Essential Dharmas may be straightforward, but they are exquisitely crafted to guide us on the path of Mahayana practice and to be applied as needed in management of the home, a company or group, or the government of a country.

In a household, all family members should be able to live without disturbance, delusion, or wrong-doing. They should always move forward with belief, zeal, questioning, and dedication. They should be grateful to one another and center their lives in self-reliance. They should always engage in learning and deepening their understanding. They should share their teaching so that others may benefit. All members should be public spirited toward the entire family. If they live this way, then the family will enjoy great grace.

This principle applies to companies and groups as well. And in governing a country, all citizens should live and work without disturbance, delusion, or wrong-doing, and people should constantly pursue belief, zeal, questioning, and dedication. Everyone should live a life of gratitude and self-reliance. They should learn, and they should teach. They should promote the public for the sake of the state. If such minds are established among its citizens, the country will prosper and be abundant with blessings.

So, the Nine Essential Dharmas of Daily Practice provide us with a marvelous method that can be used in any circumstance we encounter. Its effectiveness is guaranteed. We may take suggestions from this for our mind practice and seek out methods for managing our home, managing a company, leading a group, or ruling a country.

When we repeat these Nine Essential Dharmas over and over, practicing them constantly, we will develop our practice abilities internally, and our capabilities will develop to an unlimited degree externally. We will have greater efficiency in every workplace, be it our home or a business. We will abound with beauty and blessings.

They will provide us with a marvelous method of training to attain buddhahood and develop the ability to deliver sentient beings.

Let us consider how we might apply these Nine Essential Dharmas to the management of a business.

When the person in charge of a company practices to eliminate disturbances from the mind, she will remain unshaken by any changes, whether favorable or adverse. She will be able to fend off any winds that blow in from the outside. When she practices to eliminate delusion, she will see clearly what is essential in any action, as well as how it may benefit or harm, gain or lose, be right or wrong, and contain truth or falsehood. She will remain clear and not succumb to confusion. When she practices to eliminate wrong-doing, it will lead to the disappearance of indiscretions, corruptions, and unnecessary practices from her management, so that the right dharma, right Way, and principles live on and the great, untroubled road opens before her. When she practices to remove disbelief, greed, laziness, and ignorance, he will pursue all affairs with a critical mind-set of conviction, diligence, and questioning and a mind of consistent dedication, so there will be no stagnation in anything. She will develop a mind of gratitude and grace in whatever she encounters, drawing much assistance from others, as well as developing her own powers of autonomy, self-sufficiency, and independence and establishing a solid foundation. Her expertise will deepen as she broadens her knowledge through constant study, thereby guiding all members of her organization properly through constant teaching and leading to continued improvements in the efficiency and quality of their performance. She will promote an abundant spirit of public service, earning respect from all members of the company, which will encourage greater cooperation. When the manager does these things, the company will prosper, and her own capabilities and approach to practice will grow and change daily. This will inspire every member of her business or organization to participate with her, and thereby benefit all individuals and the group as a whole.

This is the way of Mahayana practice, which directs us towards and assures success in our practice and our work. Thus, this method, utilized properly in each and every situation, will lead to a victorious outcome.

(1) The Nine Essential Dharmas of Daily Practice

Above, I provided an overview of the Nine Essential Dharmas. I will now provide more information about their meaning, which I hope will serve as a guide for mind practitioners.

Conducting Spiritual Cultivation, Cultivation of Wisdom, Choice in Action (Articles 1, 2, and 3)

As one lives through an eternity of lives, one should establish a center. To do this, one needs concentration, wisdom, and the precepts of their true nature. When these have been substantially established, one will be able to believe in him or herself, and others will, in consequence, be able to trust in that person. One will also be able to take on any task that is presented—even matters of great significance. If one is lacking in any of these three qualities, he or she will not be grounded in belief, and others with lack trust in them. Without trust, one will not be able to undertake any work that is given.

There are things that get in the way while performing spiritual cultivation, cultivation of wisdom, and observing precepts: disturbances, delusion, and wrong-doing. When disturbances exist in our mind, we cannot establish one-pointedness of mind. When delusions are present, we are unable to establish wisdom. And when wrong-doing is present, the precepts cannot be properly established.

In general, disturbances emerge when something goes against our will or liking.

Delusion is nothing more than ignorance. It stems from a multitude of sensory conditions, but most representative are the notions of ego. When we are hindered by false notions, we become fixated. We can be blinded by this fixation. The result is ignorance. When we do not believe in the truth, we fool ourselves and others. We become prone to exaggeration regarding our capability and understanding and, with the creation of this false narrative, we engage in deceit to conceal our errors. This is where delusions originate. In Buddhism, it is said that the true buddhadharma is not becoming ensnared by anything, even by the dharma itself. Great liberation and freedom take place when we look around the void and are not bound or confined by even the slightest thing. This is when awakening happens.

There are many kinds of wrong-doing. They often result from desire. When we are filled with desire for honors, status, or objects, the "right" part of our mind collapses and wrong-doing emerges.

We need to observe the state of our mind closely. When disturbances, delusions, and wrong-doings arise, at that moment we need to return to meditation, wisdom, and the precepts to restore our original mind. It is, of course, very difficult for the beginner, who is subject to a wandering mind, to develop this understanding. Therefore, we must work from the beginning to be vigilant with our minds and use what we have established in the next stage of our practice. Eventually, we will reach the stage where restoration of our original mind comes easily and naturally without effort. Once we have reached this point in our practice, our capabilities will grow and strengthen. This is where the dharma, the Way, and all scriptures emerge.

We may separate disturbances, delusion, and wrong-doing, but succumbing to any one of them leads to the other two. They end up becoming one and the same and we create transgressive karma.

For instance, we may begin with disturbances and become mistaken and deluded. We may begin with delusion and become disturbed and mistaken. Or we may begin with wrong-doing and become deluded and disturbed.

When we succumb to disturbances and fail to achieve self-realization, this is called the ignorance of disturbances.

When we succumb to delusion and fail to achieve awareness, this is called the ignorance of delusions.

When we succumb to wrong-doing and fail to achieve awareness, this is called the ignorance of wrong-doing.

Those who succumb to these three types of ignorance will fall into the three unwholesome realms of existence

Therefore, with our disturbances, delusions, and wrong-doing, it is essential that we recover the original realm of the void and develop the capabilities of freedom.

(2) How to Confront Sensory Conditions

Sensory conditions, which manifest as attachments, aversions and discriminations that develop in our mind from past experiences, can be resources for our practice or they can become obstacles.

For our life:

As a means of study, we can examine sensory conditions as they affect others and take lessons from them. We can then apply these lessons when we face similar conditions in our own life. We can also observe their circumstances and learn how to better prepare for making our decisions.

When you encounter sensory conditions:

1. Try not to get carried away by the sensory conditions when you encounter them.
2. Stop and examine the conditions closely.
3. Study these conditions and understand the message hidden behind them.
4. After gaining this understanding, let go of everything and return to the way things were before those conditions arose. Establish a mind that is not constrained by those conditions.
5. Discover a better way to respond to conditions with a mind free from constraints.
6. Resolve all matters with a spirit of dedication and with a buddha offering. (Treat all people and situations as if they were the buddha.)

Once the sensory conditions are gone:

Assess what is right and what is wrong. Then, further develop what you did well. Search for the cause of any shortcomings and make continuous effort daily to address any weaknesses you uncover.

When we blame others for things that go awry, we miss the opportunity to develop ourselves. Blaming breeds resentment within ourselves. When we take responsibility for our choices, we move along the path to maturity.

The Three Stages of Choice based on Sound Thought

Stage 1: Stop and return to sound thought.
Stage 2: Use sound thought to make accurate judgments.
Stage 3: Choose and practice only the right actions based on your judgment.

The Nine Essential Dharmas:

The first involves establishing the equanimity of our true nature, devoting one mind to each affair, and achieving samadhi (the single pointed mind).

The second involves establishing the wisdom of our true nature, thus attaining knowledge of all affairs and universal principles and ensuring that there are no impediments.

The third involves establishing the precepts of our true nature and practicing in all matters from cultivating our personal life to regulating our household, governing the country, or keeping the world at peace.

The Threefold Practice of Non-Practitioners: Accidental, purposeless, and temporary

The Threefold Practice of Practitioners: Purposeful attainment of moral perfection in accordance with principles and moral purpose

(3) What are the Equanimity, Wisdom, and Precepts of our True Nature?

When our Equanimity, Wisdom, and Precepts are in alignment with our true nature, they are said to be our "True Nature." In other words, our original nature is not separate either in action or at rest.

Equanimity of our True Nature: The mind that establishes concentration and peace becomes one with external conditions. At this stage, a concentrated and meditative state of mind automatically manifests, even when the practitioner encounters varying sensory conditions.

Wisdom of our True Nature: The person seeking wisdom and the object that is sought are not separated. At this stage, wisdom spontaneously manifests even while sensory conditions arise.

Precepts of our True Nature: The person as subject observing the precepts, and the object disciplined by the precepts become non-dual. At this stage, precepts unconsciously manifest as sensory conditions arrive.

In this stage, our consciousness and unconsciousness become

meditative, wise, and right through the repeated training of mind practice. Consequently, the mind of the practitioner naturally and effortlessly maintains one's true nature in any situation.

Belief: The Most Vital Element in Spiritual Practice

The first three of the Nine Essential Dharmas are practiced through the Threefold Practice. If the first three essentials are viewed as three tines of a pitchfork, the fourth Essential (Belief, Zeal, Questioning, and Dedication) is the staff of the pitchfork, and it provides the driving force behind our practice.

In religion, Belief is viewed as the most important element. As stated in the dharma instruction, there are many merits in religion, including works for the order and works of charity. The principal merit among these is our ability to establish the mind of belief for someone for whom who has no belief.

The "Vein of Faith" refers to the path through which the dharma comes into our practice. The flow of the dharma through the Vein of Faith shapes our character in much the same as nutrients flow through our blood vessels. Without that path, we cannot receive even a drop of the torrential "dharma rain" that pours down upon us.

Without the Mind of Faith, we cannot begin to build even the most basic foundation. Therefore, our top priority must be to summon the mind of faith into our practice.

Some aspects of Belief and Questioning may be difficult to understand.

We typically think of Belief and Questioning as contradictory concepts; when we have a questioning mind, we do not believe and when we have faith, we do not question. Consider the concept that for every ten parts of questioning, there will be ten parts of awakening.

The "Doubt of the Fox" is doubt based in skepticism rather than belief. When we hold the doubt of the fox, we measure the teacher and the dharma, viewing ourselves as our teacher's equal and equating the merit of our own opinions with the merit of the teacher's dharma.

The character of a teacher who has achieved the status of 'Mara defeated' or higher cannot be comprehended through common-sense judgment or through the imaginings of human desires of material greed, lust, or the desire for honors and profit. The accomplished teachers are strolling in a lofty spiritual world. How can the ordinary person measure up to them with their limited capacity of intelligence and spirituality?

So "Right Belief," which is untainted by perversity or skepticism, is like the tree with its roots deep in fertile soil. The doubt of the fox is like roots that wind their way without settling into the earth. The single greatest misfortune is to harbor the 'doubt of the fox.'

Do we have right belief or the doubt of the fox?

Only when we enter the spirit of right belief, do dharma instructions enter us and become our own flesh and blood. Then, we are not constrained by ideas like "this is too difficult for me" or "I have heard this before."

The presiding Buddha's vision of loving-kindness is present in every Dharma word. We must realize this and summon forth right belief.

Zeal: The Life-Force of Our Mind

When we have confidence in something, we understand its importance. When we understand that something has real value, "Zeal" naturally emerges. The students in their studies, the scholar in research, and the entrepreneur in business cannot succeed without zeal. Without it, we have less chance of success. This is especially true when we abide by the precepts and practice with the intent to ascend to the stage of sagehood. We must generate zeal in everything we do. We need to stimulate and encourage zeal.

Zeal can be easily stifled. Should this happen, our spiritual state is like that of a rotten egg. Idleness rots the very life-force of our soul.

We encourage zeal by praising the good and punishing the bad. Praise for good deeds encourages us to exert ourselves for the good and it stimulates the life-force of zeal for the good. Punishment for bad deeds and harsh censure of evil actions restores the life-force of zeal.

When we allow ourselves to succumb to comfort and laziness, we become like the frog in a pan of cold water on the stove. It sits comfortably, unaware as the flame gradually heats the water. Before it realizes what is happening, it boils to death. We must not accept laziness and lack of zeal in others or in ourselves. Nurture zeal continuously with collective wisdom and individual practice.

Zeal also changes bad thoughts that arise at every moment into good thoughts. Zeal arises just as we experience something right or wrong. For example, just as we are about to express our mind in a reckless way, we may stop and change to a mind that responds properly. Zeal can also arise when we practice sitting meditation in the morning or at the moment we turn our distracted thoughts into right mindfulness.

We must demonstrate zeal, not only when we are engaged in some great effort, but when manifesting individual thoughts. We can direct all our thoughts to right mindfulness by assessing them and asking, "Is this a deluded thought or right mindfulness?" With every action, we rely on zeal to assess needs and distinguish whether they are right or unwise. Then, we choose the right action and make decisions for right action to benefit both the public and personal good.

Zeal also means abandoning any mistake or actions of attachment, even in very minor situations. We must allow zeal to operate in all our actions and in all our thinking.

Where zeal is absent, indecisiveness can take over. In an decisive moment, we lack the resolve to act appropriately, even though we know what is right. Our indecisiveness prevents us from doing what we must do. As a result, we succeed at nothing. In public and private affairs, we must establish a mind of zeal. A mind of zeal should be a part of our nature in everyday life. Zeal must be summoned in every aspect of our life not only for the small matters, but for the great endeavors we undertake.

For those who aspire to attain great enlightenment, zeal is a life-or-death matter. We must ask, "How am I any different from a buddha?" Resolution only comes when zeal is present in all matters, great and small.

In the beginning, zeal requires effort. If we constantly cultivate zeal, we will not need to actively summon it even when we encounter sensory conditions. Zeal will already be present for our use. When zeal becomes a habit, we achieve merit in everything we do.

Questioning: The Key to Awakening

A dharma instruction tells us that questioning is the primary motivating force in learning what we do not know.

Keep in mind that the more advanced and intelligent a living creature is, the more questioning and inquiry it displays.

Knowledge comes when we ask questions. We develop as people as we experience awakening. If this does not happen, we will be unable to transcend a merely biological existence.

Sages ask questions. So do ordinary humans that have a critical mind-set. Through questioning, their tomorrows evolve from their todays. They develop to such a degree that they may question whether it is all just an illusion. The person who lives one's life with a questioning mind constantly transforms his life.

Of course, there are questions that everyone asks. We all have questions associated with our own area of interest: artists have questions about art, philosophers about philosophy. Questions are like flashlights: we shine them toward the things we are curious about and they light up for us. In that way, an object of curiosity becomes fully illuminated.

In our practice, we pose questions as a way of awakening to the truth. These include questions of awakening, as well as personal questions.

When a scientist invents something, he or she starts by making a hypothesis. One may not be able to see or hear electricity, but may hypothesize that positive and negative charges must exist, and that the two will cause a light to shine when they meet. He studies the phenomenon until it finally becomes clear, and that's when the invention comes.

Hypotheses that do not conform to the natural laws will never be realized. We may hypothesize that we can make rice cakes out of rocks, but this will never happen, no matter how hard we try. We need to make hypotheses that conform to the principles based on what is true, and concentrate on questions that are based on those principles. Only these questions produce sound results.

Questions based in belief come from making the right hypotheses—even if we are uncertain—and they will ultimately lead us to awakening. When disbelief underlies our questions, the answers will only move us farther and farther away.

It is important to trust in dharma instructions as spoken by the sages and saints. Keep a questioning mind with a sense of dedication. This includes matters of right and wrong or gain and loss.

If we harbor questions with a mind of greed or harming others, they will lead us to commit grave transgressions with fearsome karmic consequences. When we consider questions to the end, with a mind of service to others, we will achieve awakening to the correct solution.

When we perform human affairs with a mind of service, everything becomes a blessing and merit. Saving lives becomes a merit, giving praise becomes a merit, even scolding becomes a merit.

When we harbor questions with the intent of harming others, even the praise we offer will lack virtue. The virtue drains away when we speak ill of others. Our words should always be words of service.

If they are not, they become harmful and may ultimately lead us into transgressions.

Only when we proceed with questions based in belief, sound principles, and a mind of service, does the path become a gateway of blessings.

It is said that we should consider questions like a hen brooding an egg. She does so with such devotion that she avoids eating until she absolutely must. She ignores her biological needs until the last moment. When she does go out, she takes care of her needs all at once, eating quickly and returning to her brood. For ten to fifteen days, she does the same exact thing. Finally, after 21 days, the chick pecks through from the inside and the hen pecks through from the outside. At last, a new life is born.

No one succeeds at anything by considering questions only once or twice. Awakening only comes when the process of our questioning mind is complete. It is like the eggshell that remains impenetrable through the 19th and 20th day, only to break apart on the 21st. The path to realization comes when a well-considered opportunity provides a way.

It is said that Sakyamuni Buddha awakened to the way when he saw a star in the morning sky. This was not because some universal principle of large and small, being and nonbeing, was present in the star. It was an occasion that provided the starting point for him to achieve awakening with a question that he had already been contemplating.

No one lives without questions. When we hold and contemplate questions that arise in our minds, we gain clarity and broaden our perspective. Our inner spiritual questions lead us to understanding we never had before. These spiritual questions illuminate the internal world of our mind and the principles of our true nature. We can also keep questions concerning how we might serve and help others. Let us deeply consider the question of what we as practitioners can do to truly serve ourselves and others.

Dedication: Essential Element of Success

Those who read the dharma instructions, yet fail to incorporate them into their character will experience misfortune, even when they proceed to the next world. Practitioners need to recite the Essential Dharmas of Daily Practice in the morning and evening. The content is not difficult to understand. They are relatively short. It is beneficial to practice each one, making them a part of ourselves. Dedication makes this possible.

Dedication refers to an unremitting state of mind—a mind that follows through. Those who are dedicated do not give up on what they have started. Once they have begun something, they continue until it is completed with the desired result. *Dedication* allows us to achieve our goal. If belief represents the roots, dedication is the deep roots the plant need to bear fruit. Once we have firmly established steadfast belief and dedication, a consecration ceremony and celebration are held for us in the pure dharma realm.

Attaining buddhahood is guaranteed if we establish a mind of faith, dedication and spiritual strength. Without dedication, we will see no fruit. We must have dedication that endures until the end and inspires us to do whatever is necessary to achieve our goal.

In *The Doctrine of the Mean*, we find the words, "Dedication is the way of the heavens. The attainment of dedication is the path." Sincere dedication never wavers, not even for a moment. It is constant, continuing throughout the day and night for all seasons. This is the mark of 'perfect dedication.'

The way of man proceeds with sincerity and dedication. This means that we should always walk with sincere commitment as we seek the way of heaven.

The same book tells us that if just one ordinary person succeeds in a single effort through study, inquiry, reflection, discriminating clearly, and practicing earnestly, then a superior person will make a hundred efforts. It maintains, if one succeeds with ten efforts, the superior person will succeed with a thousand efforts. In doing so, their ignorance will surely turn to awareness, and their weakness turn to strength.

We also hear of utter persistence and exactitude. This is referring to the thoroughness and consistency of sincere dedication. If zeal is the starting point, then dedication is the perseverance that we show in carrying through to the end. Even if belief, zeal, and questioning are present, we will see no results without dedication. Therefore, we must incorporate this dedication practice into our very being if we are to realize the fruits of our efforts in public and personal affairs.

This combination of belief, zeal, questioning, and dedication is the way to progress toward awakening and entering the Way. We should therefore guard this carefully without fail. Disbelief, greed, laziness, and ignorance are conditions that work against awakenings. They should therefore be completely abandoned. Right belief can only take hold when a great aspirational force is present. It is only when belief has emerged that zeal arises. We require zeal for there to be questions that we cannot let go. Only when we focus on great and urgent questions does sincere dedication emerge. It is from this unremitting dedication that we attain awakening.

Therefore, the practitioner of the Way must be on guard against disbelief, greed, laziness, and ignorance. One must apply great devotion to establish the virtues of belief, zeal, questioning and dedication.

The practice of Won-Buddhism emphasizes perseverance. Those who diligently and truthfully carry out a daily routine will experience maturation of spirit and derive merit that will transform their practice as well as their daily lives.

Therefore, when we regard our daily life as an opportunity for practice and approach it with an awakened mind, our practice becomes easier and more convenient. It is simply a matter of living an ordinary life. Our practice strengthens as we treat our affairs with a one-pointed mind. This guides us toward a level of maturity where our powers of Spiritual Cultivation, Cultivation of Wisdom and Inquiry, and Choice in Action accumulate.

Dharma Words on Dedication

1. We, and all things in the universe, are formed through initiation, execution, and conclusion. This is done with dedication.
2. "Dedication" here means choosing a strong vow and holding on to it firmly without letting go. We do extensive study on

the important affairs that we undertake; we inquire closely, we reflect carefully, and we practice earnestly.

3. From dedication derives truth, purity, oneness, consistency, persistence, completeness, and earnestness without fail.

4. Where there is utter dedication, even solid rock is penetrated, and even the most impregnable of gates is opened.

5. Utter dedication has no in or out, beginning or end. It is uniform and neither rests nor ceases.

6. All objects in the world are created through dedication. There is nothing in nature or man that succeeds without dedication.

7. This universe is a mass of dedication. All things in it are the result of dedication. Nothing in this world is anything other than a by-product of dedication.

8. When we arrive at a state of utter dedication, the radiance appears like the divine brightness of heaven and earth. None of the world's rising and falling, prosperity or decline, can exist outside its field of vision.

9. Once absorbed in utter dedication, one is part of the transformation and growth of heaven and earth.

10. When great dedication is present, there is nothing that we cannot do. Procrastination and laziness disappear when great dedication is present.

Turning to a Life of Gratitude

If everything in the world is formed through mutual relationships of grace, then grace will grow to limitless abundance in this world.

When the ties of grace are cut, our very lifeline has been severed.

Acknowledging the path of the Fourfold Grace opens the bright Way of eternal life for practitioners.

This practice is set forth in the Essential Dharmas of Daily Practice: "Let us turn a life of resentment into a life of gratitude."

When times are good, we create a corresponding life-giving response. When we live recklessly, we create harm and make enemies. What must we do to turn every situation into grace? We experience gratitude for positive relationships. Can we resolve those cases where resentment has built up over weeks and years? Can we turn these into grace by repaying them with gratitude? Also, we should consider how to avoid producing resentment and how to discover gratitude even when we encounter unfavorable conditions.

Resentment that has built up over eons and lifetimes is not easily resolved even through buddha offerings in this life.

It is so difficult that we may end up saying that hateful people have nothing attractive about them at all. We may even hate them when they do kind things: When they make food. When they laugh. When they come and go. We may hate everything about them.

If we want to be assured of eternal life, we must cleanse ourselves thoroughly with practice and turn from a life of resentment to a life of gratitude, even in difficult situations. If we do not, we are certain to experience internal torment and create harm for ourselves and others. In addition, we will surely encounter those same difficulties again at a later point in time.

Sakyamuni Buddha said that when he practiced as a hermit in one of his previous lives, he did not harbor even the slightest resentment or anger, even as the King of Kalinga severed his hands and feet. He described his feelings by saying, "The man who knows does not blame the fool. How can I blame the King of Kalinga for what he does out of ignorance?" He bore no anger or resentment under the circumstances, no matter how bad the conditions.

If we want to be assured of eternal life, we must never lose this mindset of turning a life of resentment into a life of gratitude. The following nine questions about showing gratitude provide a way to cleanse ourselves.

Nine Questions about Showing Gratitude

1. Have I discovered every element of grace offered to me and am I grateful for it?
2. Do I experience the Fourfold Grace in my life? Do all my actions express my gratitude?
3. Do I maintain an outlook of gratitude even when adverse conditions torment me or threaten my existence? Can I remain composed and never experience even a hint of resentment?
4. Am I capable of resolving resentments that have built up over the course of lifetimes and turn them into grace?
5. Do I have enough generosity to grant forgiveness a hundred times for a hundred errors and turn them into grace?
6. Do I have confidence in my ability to maintain this grace through an eternity of lifetimes?
7. Can I use all favorable and adverse conditions as well as all good and bad affinities to express grace?

8. Can I create grace for all worlds and all sentient beings and change harm into life-giving benefits for every living creature?
9. Can I discover limitless grace in the myriad objects of heaven and earth, the empty dharma realm, and all things in the world, cultivating and use it without exception?

Requital of the Fourfold Grace is:

A path that connects moral sensibilities with all things in the universe

A path that makes grace of all things in the universe

A path that makes good affinities of all things in the universe

A path that makes a field of blessings from all things in the universe.

Turning to a Life of Self-Reliance

Master Daesan, the Third Head Dharma Master of Won-Buddhism, gave a dharma instruction on the direction we should take in developing self-power. He said we should follow a threefold effort to develop **autonomy of the spirit, financial independence,** and **physical self-reliance**. The last two are important, but autonomy of the spirit is fundamental. It is through the autonomy of spirit that all our capabilities are developed. When it is present, we can use wit, beauty, fame, and fortune in ways that are positive for the world. If autonomy of the spirit has not been established, then, we will lose all our wit, beauty, fame, and fortune.

The exercise of spiritual autonomy means to not curry favor with others, protect their egos, or simply do as they tell us. Similarly, it means not being bound by regulations or engaging in things because we have no choice in the matter. In short, it means we must discover and pursue our own right path and blaze our own trails in all our undertakings. When we have the autonomy to take care of ourselves, reliance on others transforms into self-reliance. This relates to every aspect of our lives. If we do not live a life of self-reliance, we may lose our independence.

We also need to develop self-reliance when dealing with other people. Complete dependence on others is unwise. It will only hinder the development of self-reliance.

Personal development, the development of a group or community, and the development of a country all depend upon our ability to develop independence and self-reliance. The principal self-reliance of the spirit is one where we seek to cultivate our own destiny rather than putting it in the hands of others. We want to develop self-reliance not because a life of self-reliance is in itself a good thing. Rather, we must forge a future that is independent of the fluctuations of the world. Our fortunes must not hinge on the rise and fall, prosperity and decline, calamity and happiness or fortune and misfortune of others.

When we have practiced a life of self-reliance again and again, it becomes instilled within us. We arrive at a stage where things naturally develop and resolve on their own accord. This marks the moment when total independence in practice has been established.

When self-reliance has become an iron pillar at the center, with a stone wall surrounding it on all sides; when we reach the stage where our mind is not moved by wealth and honor or swayed by weapons and power; then we have attained a complete self-reliance that everyone can trust.

When we reach the stage where we can resolve any issue through self-reliance, self-reliance extends outward to everything. This is not the kind of self-reliance that runs out if we do not replenish it. This self-reliance replenishes itself. It becomes a limitless driving force that enables us to succeed in everything we do.

The Ways of Self-Power and Other-Power

1. We live an eternal life through self-power and other-power. This has been an ironclad rule since the beginning of time.
2. Self-power is life, our true nature, and a limitless driving force.
3. We gain independence when we establish self-power and forfeit independence when we lose self-power.
4. Self-power is the foundation for other-power, and other-power is the foundation for self-power.
5. When we have self-power, other-power turns into self-reliance. When we lack self-power, we cannot sustain even our own life.
6. When we lack self-power, even a mountain of other-power is useless. When we lack other-power, even a great pine tree of self-power will eventually wither and die.
7. Those who focus solely on self-power may fall victim to arrogance and lose balance. Those who focus solely on other-power can easily succumb to lethargy and collapse from exhaustion.
8. We use other-power to build our self-power and we invest our self-power to build greater self-reliance.
9. Therefore, we must combine self-power with other-power to

develop financial independence, physical self-reliance, and spiritual autonomy.

10. We must contribute to society to repay what we received. The farther those contributions reach, the more our ability to be self-reliant grows.

This principle applies equally to individuals, societies, organizations, religious groups, and nations. Let us awaken to this fact, nurture our self-power, and make practical use of other-power.

Turning to a Willingness to Learn Well

Anyone who commands their true nature and conducts human affairs well is our teacher. Anyone whose handling of human affairs is superior to our own, whose knowledge of life is superior to our own, or whose scholarship and technical skills are superior to our own is our teachers. We cannot become a wise person without learning from teachers.

Sotaesan, the Founding Master of Won-Buddhism, said that learning from everyone we meet broadens our knowledge. Even though he was an all-knowing sage, he recognized the need to constantly learn. Similarly, Confucius said, "There are only two things: do not reject learning, and do not neglect teaching."

This idea of turning a reluctance to learn into a willingness to learn well is based on the principle of the primacy of the wise. The reluctance to learn from the wise, arises from an abundance of pride and too much ego. If we refuse to acknowledge anything other than what we know, our pride will hold us back. Therefore, we must set aside our position and age, our prestige and pride, and adopt an open-minded view to learning new things.

For those who have a mind open to learning, this world is an endless ground of enlightenment.

The endless flood of information and news that dominates our ever-changing, modern society threatens to overwhelm us. If we instill a willingness to learn through the entirety of our lives, we will develop an adaptive ability to navigate the present-day overflow of information. The same is true for knowledge of life, for our academic studies, and for common wisdom. When we neglect to learn because we believe we already have the answers, we risk misfortune for lifetimes. Wisdom becomes more radiant as we cultivate it and knowledge builds as we accumulate it.

Even a wise person may find himself slipping into foolishness when he does not realize he is being foolish; even a foolish person becomes wiser when he understands that he is being foolish. This is an obvious truth. Arrogance, based on a fixed notion of knowing, is not a proper approach to practice.

Socrates instructed his students to understand their own ignorance. How frustrated he must have been to see how unaware they were of how little they knew. Their first step toward wisdom was to understand the limits of their knowledge. We must recognize where we are ignorant. Instead of rushing to excuses or denial, we need to strive to learn. Our approach should be one of an unceasing willingness to learn across the eternity of our lives. This includes the world of truth, the world of commanding our true nature, and the everyday world.

We encourage plants to grow by giving them water and fertilizer; a person cannot grow without learning. You may believe that you will grow naturally, but if you do not learn humbly, you will only see the idea of the self, growing ever higher like a mountain.

Therefore, we must resist being taken in by our own pride. Instead, we should instill in ourselves a willingness to learn from anyone and make this a habit that extends through all our lives.

Turning to a Willingness to Teach Well

Among the dharma instructions of Master Chongsan, the Second Head Dharma Master of Won-Buddhism, there is an admonition to encourage the good and punish the bad in one another. This is a vital instruction that exhorts us to learn and teach throughout our lives.

The term "teaching" carries several meanings. Among them is the education of the children of others. Primarily, the meaning lies in educating people to correct any deficiencies or ignorance, even if we just start with people around us such as our friends and neighbors.

No one can become a leader without teaching. In fact, we only become leaders when we teach well. Our leadership capabilities cannot grow unless we have expertise in teaching. When we teach consistently, we develop a multitude of abilities that allow us to help even the most stubborn sentient being.

A society where the grace of teaching flourishes will naturally develop into a place of productivity, efficiency, and moral strength, a community where every matter is resolved with grace.

There is hope for society through the examples of learning and teaching set by practitioners. Veterans teach newcomers, but the newcomers also teach the veterans. Thus, the grace of teaching grows richer as it expands from the bottom to the top.

No one learns to swim by theory alone. If we don't ever get in the water and try to swim, we will never succeed. We may buy a car and study driving, but until we set it on the road, we will never know how to drive.

The same applies to any form of knowledge; we must try and teach it before we can truly know it. If we experience arrogance, then that will interfere with our learning and teaching. We really must understand the damage that arrogance does.

In the *Book of Changes*, the lesson on the virtue of humility teaches the following: The way of heaven lowers the arrogant and aids the humble. The law of earth causes changes in the arrogant and pushes them toward humility. The spirits harm the arrogant and bless the humble. The ways of man resent the arrogant and favor the humble.

When we let go of arrogance and adopt humility, our light will shine even in the highest of places No one will dare underrate us, even when we are down at the bottom. In everything we do, we must seek out and discard anything cold or distant or conceited in our heart and mind.

Therefore, when we turn a reluctance to teach into a willingness to teach others and ourselves, the grace of teaching will abound and we will become leaders possessing a multitude of abilities that allow us to deliver all living creatures.

The Way of Teaching and Learning

1. True growth and development in any individual or group is fostered by learning and teaching.
2. We cannot become a wise person if we do not learn. We cannot become a leader unless we teach.
3. In every field, from commanding our true nature and human morality, to scholarship, technology, affairs of state, everyday life, and common wisdom, we should strive to learn all that we can from those who have more knowledge or skill than we do.
4. Where we find those with less knowledge or skill, we should go to them and offer teaching. We incur a debt when we merely know and do not teach. We must offer teaching that clarifies, awakens, and corrects.
5. No practitioner should approach a superior or inferior with a judgmental mind.
6. When we learn and teach with a practicing mind, great practice will open and great capabilities will surge forth.
7. A sage once said: "do not reject learning, and do not neglect teaching."
8. When we envy the wisdom and abilities of others, we are unable to improve ourselves. When we admire wisdom and take pleasure in the good, we can handle any matter under the sun.
9. There is no distinction of self and other in learning and teaching. There is no male or female, young or old, good or bad, wisdom or foolishness, high or low, left or right, rich or poor, noble or common.

10. For the sake of learning, we must let go of our ideas and prejudices and open our mind to learning well.

Turning Toward an Eagerness for the Public's Welfare

When we embrace the spirit of public service, we move beyond the sense of individual need and that of our own family. Instead, we engage in acts of Mahayana altruism from a broader perspective for all sentient beings.

What meaning does such a spirit hold today?

Since the collapse of imperialism and totalitarianism, a wave of belief in liberty and human rights has swept over all of us. Our world has truly become a world where humans are freed from the longstanding chains and can finally stand free. It is a truly great change, one that is worthy of celebration.

But new side effects have emerged from these human rights and freedoms. Public spirit eroded tremendously as human rights devolved into selfishness and liberty slided into unrestrained debauchery.

It would be impossible to list all the social pathologies that have resulted from the use of official undertakings for private gain, embezzlement, fraud, corruption, destruction of the public order, and breaches of public law. If we consider the resulting direct and indirect damages, we see that it is a seriously tragic situation, to say the least.

These trends provide a sickness in our hearts and minds, impacting on the public spirit. This dharma instruction admonishing us to "turn lack of public spirit into an eagerness for the public's welfare" has an even more urgent meaning to it now.

Let us examine what is meant by "public" and "private."

Dharma Words on the Public and Private

1. The public and private are different yet one, one yet different.
2. There can be no private without the public, nor public without the private.
3. If we preserve the public, the private can also survive.
4. Since we must preserve the private, we must preserve the public.
5. The best approach is one that allows both public and private to survive.
6. Selfishness consists in conspiring to achieve private gains at the expense of the public.
7. Totalitarianism consists in unjustly focusing solely on the public with the assumption that the private is to be sacrificed.
8. Nothing private can be sacrificed without the principles of public law, nor can anything public be advocated when the private is involved.
9. A democratic system is based on majority rule. However, it should not tolerate the abuses toward the few by the majority.
10. Personal freedoms should be guaranteed, but we cannot allow unrestrained self-indulgence. Human rights should be guaranteed, but we cannot permit acts of harm against others.
11. The public may become private when it is used for private purposes, but even personal affairs become public when utter impartiality and selflessness are achieved.
12. We must bring about a process of maturation, by moving from

a perspective that puts private before the public, to one that considers public and private equally important, and eventually to a perspective that places the needs of the public before the private, in order to be of service with utter impartiality and selflessness.

It is said in the dharma instructions that the public spirit can only emerge when one's mind is devoid of selfishness and that one can be unified with the whole only if one is filled with a public spirit. When we have a public spirit, we may suffer harm and face desperate situations, yet we will have a mind that never permits us to harm the public or break its household's rules. Yet if we observe institutions that generate a lot of commotion and direct misleading claims toward the public, we find that a great deal of the influence behind their actions is derived from the private sector, lurking just beneath the surface.

Those with a strong public spirit become one with the cause that is aligned with the community's interest. They become united as a matter of course. It is only by uniting that we become an agent of harmony throughout the ten directions of the world.

In the days ahead, there will be no place for ventures that are designed purely for personal gain that damage the public's interest. Their success will be determined by how broad their spirit of public service is and how noble their public values are. An age is at hand where we will need to conduct ourselves with a mind of public service, rather than living and prospering with a mind of selfishness. In this way we will be acknowledged by the world. This does not mean that we are to serve only the public, while sacrificing all our personal matters.

Rather, we should work for the public so that we may live as it thrives, and the public thrives as we thrive. It is with this spirit that we should guide the world.

The public spirit encompasses several distinct forms: the speculative public spirit, as well as the public spirit of speech, action, vision, and spontaneous transformation. If we work ceaselessly to develop our public spirit and exalt the spirit of public service in a healthy manner, we will enter a paradise replete with the grace of the public interest. The leaders in such a world will be those whose spirit of public service is thorough.

The Path of Selfless Service

1. If we wish to make this world a better place, we will have to work together and share this great responsibility. Where many such people exist, there is hope, light, and honor.
2. When a person with a responsible nature and a spirit of selfless service ventures out in search of work to do, they accomplish all their endeavors without the concern for credit or praise.
3. Such a person understands that all people are of one family and therefore assumes responsibility for the care of all sentient beings.
4. When one regards the suffering and pleasure of others as one's own, endless comfort, encouragement, and assistance are realized.
5. When one focuses on tending to everything oneself without any expectation of help from others, others will naturally hold them in high regard and be grateful for their help.

6. Such a person assumes responsibility, credits those who help him, treats others in an uncalculating way, and accepts his responsibilities with a simple sense of duty.
7. One observes each situation and offers encouragement to those who are working, inspiration to those who are not, and help those who are frustrated and need encouragement and hope to rise again.
8. Whenever such a person sees misfortune or error, they take steps to help by encouraging the good and warning against the bad. The more difficult things are, the more they try to offer assistance and support.
9. Such a person works to unite people for a greater public spirit. Establishing fair rules and discovering ways to direct a positive and successful outcome through harmony and cooperation.
10. One is endlessly serving, awakening, and guiding people onto the right path. That person is consistently working with others to build a paradise on earth.
11. Blessings naturally follow to those who work for the benefit of all people.

Such a person will pay homage to the heavens, earth, and humankind,
Do the work of heaven and earth,
By guiding and leading all beings in heaven and earth,
And present a grand vision of governance
To the limitless world.

Admonitions from the Doctrine

1. When we pay back grace with gratitude, harm transforms into grace. When we are resentful and ungrateful, grace transforms into harm.
2. When we have self-reliance, even other-reliance becomes self-reliance. However, when we lack self-reliance, we cannot sustain the self-reliance we have.
3. In a society where the wise are assured a place suited to the wise, the way is opened for the flourishing of wise man and fool alike. Should the wise fall to the station of a fool and the foolish rise to the station of the wise, both the foolish and wise will suffer humiliation and society will collapse.
4. Where there is education, there is a bright future. Where there is no education, only darkness lies ahead. The smallest droplet of water can form a tidal wave of benefit to society.
5. In a society where the public-spirited are venerated, all of us may be saved by grace. In a society where the public-spirited are persecuted, no one escapes the snare of torment. When we proclaim the greatness of the small, a radiant life is assured for great and small alike. When we proclaim the smallness of the great, only darkness awaits.
6. For those who have the power of spiritual cultivation, any sensory condition that arises has no more effect than a mild breeze or a tiny insect. But for those who lack the power of Cultivation, the most insignificant condition will roar like a lion or blow like a hurricane.

7. Those who have the power of Wisdom and Inquiry will experience greater development and advancement as they tackle increasingly difficult challenges. But those who lack the power of wisdom and inquiry will panic facing the simplest problems and stir up great clouds over trivial matters.
8. Those with the power of Choice in Action will advance and progress with every situation. Those who lack this power will experience nothing but frustration in every situation.
9. When the Four Articles to Develop (faith, zeal, questioning mind, and dedication) are present, we see only advancement even amid the slings and arrows of misfortune. When the Four Articles to Forsake (disbelief, greed, laziness, and ignorance) are present, we see only regression and failure even when favorable winds are present. We will never attain buddhahood with the Four Articles to Forsake.
10. The flaws in our character dig traps in our future.

The Ultimate Stage of Practice with the Nine Essential Dharmas

1. Neither shaken nor tainted even when we are surrounded by wit, beauty, fame, fortune, or any type of favorable or adverse sensory conditions.
2. Neither lost nor bewildered even when amid the confusion of great and small, being and nonbeing, right and wrong, gain and loss.
3. Neither changing nor crumbling, even when faced with great

matters of gain and loss, suffering and happiness, or when birth and death are at stake.

4. Possessing belief, zeal, questioning, and dedication that have the capacity to overcome any barrier, guiding all to success.

5. Repaying grace with gratitude so that grace arises without regret, even when resentment has built over many lifetimes.

6. Developing self-reliance into a force that emerges for all living creatures.

7. Willingness to learn from the wise, removing any sense of status, age, experience, and pride.

8. Possessing a leadership ability to guide all living creatures in an endlessly confusing world toward awakening.

9. Maintaining utter impartiality and selflessness, even amid tyranny and human ignorance.

The Roots, Branches, and Sequence of the Essential Dharmas

1. The Essential Way of Practice is the path of self-cultivation. The Essential Way of Human Life is the path for us to walk as noble human beings. We must use these two main principles together. We should use the Essential Way of Practice as our basis as we follow the Essential Way of Human Living.

2. We must pursue the Threefold Practice in tandem: with Spiritual Cultivation as the roots, Cultivation of Wisdom and Inquiry, the flowers, and Choice in Action, as the fruit.

3. Practice is a battle between the Four Articles to Develop and

the Four Articles to Forsake. The Four Articles to Forsake are naturally extinguished when the Four Articles to Develop are at work. Our vow provides an unlimited motivating force behind the Four Articles to Develop.

4. We must discover human grace. It is essential that we delve deeper into the source of that grace. When we do so, all things in the universe, favorable or adverse, become living grace.

5. We must develop self-reliance. But it is also necessary to make use of the strength of others. While both self-power and other-power are necessary, self-power comes first.

6. We must learn and teach, but learning must come first. Once we have learned; we must teach. Then, our capabilities will continuously develop without limitation.

7. In final analysis, the development of self-reliance and self-management in public service are the essential preconditions. Once we have developed them, we can serve the public effectively.

8. If we intend to follow the Essential Way of Practice, we must resolutely enter the Gateway of Practice. If we intend to follow the Essential Way of Human Life, we must resolutely enter the Gateway of Faith. If we merely wander outside the gateway, we will never get near the essence.

"If you read and put into practice 'The Essential Dharmas of Daily Practice' your whole life, that will be sufficient for attaining buddhahood."

— *"Dharma Admonitions," from The Dharma Words of Master Chongsan*

How to Attain the Three Great Powers of the Mind

From the moment we are born into this world, we live between action and rest. *Action* describes those times when we are busy with events in our lives, while *rest* refers to occasions when we have no matters to deal with and are simply living and resting.

Taken together, action and rest describe the entirety of our lives. In other words, a living person is either in action or at rest. We are either moving or not moving. Of course, our actions inevitably take on many different forms. Likewise, every period of rest is unique. Our times of rest are similar in that we are not active, but the circumstances are always different.

Since our lives are made up of either action or rest, one or the other, how do we use both in our practice? These words truly get to the heart of our practice, because we cannot practice outside action and rest. Therefore, the wise and proper approach uses the respective characteristics of both action and rest as the material of practice.

So far, my intention has been to help you understand the nature of the mind and to point out the tasks that confront us. If you understand sufficiently, the question of how to promote the three great powers of the mind (The Power of Spiritual Cultivation, The Power of Wisdom and Inquiry, The Power of Choice in Action) emerges as the primary point of interest.

Currently, there are a great many groups and organizations in the world that instruct people in different methods of practice. Whatever the method, purposeful practice of any of them will probably produce positive results. This presumes an understanding of the principles that constitute the true essence of practice. Practitioners should remain faithful to the great principle of the twofold practice. We should be wary of those who opt for only one method and proclaim it to be the only correct method of practice.

Since our true nature is not confined to any single framework, we must strive to cultivate it in various ways to develop the ability to adapt to any circumstance. If we restrict ourselves to just one method to cultivate our true nature, we will cultivate that area, but we also leave other areas completely uncultivated, remaining incapable of adjusting to changes in our environment.

Therefore, two-fold cultivation is the foundation of practice. The result of this two-fold cultivation is known as mastering the Way. As a simultaneous practice of universal principles and human affairs, and simultaneous cultivation of concentration and wisdom, the pursuit of the Threefold Practice in tandem, and two-fold cultivation are essential.

These days, we hear about all sorts of different forms of practice—so many that I could never list them all. We hear of awareness practice, thought-shedding practice, thought-watching practice, concentrating on a single object, working with a koan, practice with cutting off all sight and hearing for long periods of sitting up straight, and extreme ascetic practice.

We might decide to examine all these types of practice and test them to find their strengths and weaknesses. Eventually, we would settle on one of them. We could waste an entire lifetime wandering from method to method. It is not important that we extensively examine every available method of practice. Instead, we should understand the principle of our own nature and engage in a practice that is well suited to the characteristics of our true nature. This approach allows us to engage in proper practice without needless wandering.

The *Quickest Expedient to Attain the Three Great Powers in Action and at Rest* was developed in consideration of all these factors.

Sotaesan, the Founding Master of Won-Buddhism suggested:

"The quickest expedients for practitioners to attain the power of Cultivation in both action and rest are as follows. First, in all your actions, do nothing that will disturb or devastate your spirit and avoid such sensory conditions. Second, do not entertain craving or greed in responding to any matter. Instead, habituate yourself to having a dispassionate attitude. Third, when you are doing one thing, don't be distracted by something else, so that you concentrate only on the task at hand. Fourth, in your spare time, pay attention to reciting the buddha's name or sitting in meditation.

"The quickest expedients for attaining the power of Inquiry in both action and rest are as follows. First, in all your actions, strive to gain knowledge regarding each situation that you encounter. Second, strive to exchange opinions with teachers and colleagues. Third, when doubt arises while you are seeing, listening, or thinking, strive to resolve your doubts by following the proper order of inquiry. Fourth, strive diligently to deepen your acquaintance with our scriptures. Fifth, after deepening your acquaintance with our scriptures, broaden your knowledge and perspective by consulting the scriptures of all previous religious schools.

"The quickest expedients for attaining the power of Choice in both action and rest are as follows. First, once you know something is right, proceed with it even at the risk of your life, regardless of whether it is great or small. Second, once you know something is wrong, desist from it even at the risk of your life, regardless of whether it is great or small. Third, in all your actions, do not be discouraged even when the power of Choice does not come readily, but persist in your sincere effort and endlessly accumulate the virtues of practice."

Overcoming Difficult Hurdles

There is a supremely difficult barrier that arises as we practice according to the principles described above. It is a barrier that exists for all of us, although it is never the same for any two people. It may differ based on our spiritual capacity. It may arise several times or appear just once before going away. Some of us have the greatest difficulty, while others overcome it with ease. This is because we have all learned different things over the course of our past and we all have different spiritual capacities. Regardless of the effort required, we must overcome this obstacle.

When we run up against such a barrier, it is very easy to give up hope, to fret over how imposing it seems to be, or to wander around aimlessly, questioning whether to continue or not. The challenge is rooted in our view that these barriers are ineradicable, unknowable and impossible to overcome. In these moments, we must gather our courage to turn reluctance into determination and hesitation into action. Only then can we bring our full capabilities to bear against even the most formidable obstacle.

Ably Eradicating the Ineradicable

We must clear away things that resist clearing away, ridding ourselves of them completely, until we arrive at the stage where there is nothing left to remove.

Ably Knowing the Unknowable

We must examine things that are difficult to understand, resolutely investigating them until we arrive at the stage of complete and penetrating knowledge of them.

Ably Doing the Undoable

When it is difficult for us to act, we must take action capably, resolutely and thoroughly, until we arrive at the stage where we succeed of our own accord even when we do not make an effort.

What does "ably eradicating the ineradicable" mean?

We tend to disregard trivial things and wave them off easily. Other things resist being waved off, disregarded or cleared away. These barriers vary in their underlying nature. They may be instinctual. They may represent karmic obstacles. They may be habitual. They may be related to right and wrong or gain and loss. They may be philosophical or ethical. Or they may be something else altogether. Nevertheless, the are all defilements.

When we boldly strive to shake off, erase, abandon, and clear away anything that resists removal, according to our spiritual capacity, our soul becomes pure. Our liberation abilities are developed. And the great power of samadhi takes shape.

Therefore, when we find something is difficult to clear away, we must constantly engage in practice with the resolution to clear it away.

What does "ably knowing the unknowable" mean?

This means to capably, resolutely, and thoroughly investigate those things that resist understanding. One old saying goes, "There are things that are difficult for a single ordinary human or sentient being to understand and do well, but when we arrive at that extreme, there are things that even the sages cannot understand or do well."

When faced with extreme conditions, we may feel like we are wandering about in a fog, unsure how to proceed. This does not only happen in extreme situations. It can also happen with everyday occurrences that unfold according to the principles of great and small, being and nonbeing, right and wrong, or gain and loss. Even mundane affairs can serve as a koan. So, it should be no surprise that particularly complex or sublime situations may seem beyond our ability to understand.

Everything in the world is open to questioning for those who are prepared to work diligently to understand even the most difficult questions When we carry around questions, doing whatever it takes to understand them, we will finally arrive at an awakening. When we overlook small questions without making them subjects for questioning, we miss the opportunity for understanding them.

So, no matter how difficult or unclear something may be, when it serves as a koan and we seek to understand at all costs, we may finally arrive at the stage of knowing the unknowable.

What does "ably doing the undoable" mean?

This means to act decisively when action seems impossible. However trivial and routine something may be, we must make a special effort to act in accordance with desirable ideas, rules, and regulations. This would be utterly impossible if we were to approach living with reckless abandon. When we make the vow to engage in practice toward shedding the flaws of a sentient being, attaining buddahood, and ascending to the rank of buddha-bodhisattva and sage, we must expect difficulties and failures to arise in our path. Of course, they will be present.

A great deal of conflict may arise when we experience difficulties or failure. When things are not achieved as we had hoped, the way ahead becomes unclear. We may consider turning back and giving up in the face of a seemingly inescapable dilemma. However, in one corner of our mind, we will have the thought that we cannot give up now, even as all the minions of Mara do their worst to us.

Take the following to heart when faced with such a dilemma: "If another succeeds in one try, I will try a hundred times. If another succeeds after ten tries, I will try a thousand times." If we bring this spirit to our dilemma, we will eventually enjoy success with even the most difficult challenges.

These moments demand great zeal and resolution. We must let go of everything so we may boldly and courageously devote ourselves to resolute action and exertion to move forward and accumulate merit.

This is what is meant by "ably doing the undoable."

It means boldly carrying out what seems impossible.

When we do the undoable, the laurel crown of victory is ours. However, if we fail to do so, we are defeated and may race toward regression.

Therefore, when we face this necessary hurdle in our practice and acquire the three great powers of the mind, then we must boldly surmount it by:

ably eradicating the ineradicable,
ably knowing the unknowable,
and ably doing the undoable.

In doing so, we will surely gain the wish-fulfilling gem, let loose a cry of victory, and sing a song of exaltation as we enjoy the unending satisfaction of ascending to the lotus platform.

… Part III

The Reality of Spiritual Cultivation

In previous sections, I provided an overview of the mind and stated the necessary principles for our practice. A general understanding of the basics of practice should be clear before we question how true spiritual cultivation begins. True cultivation is not resolved through abstract intellectual thinking, rather it is cultivated through concrete and realistic spiritual practice.

At this point, I would like to include an explanation of the specific steps we should take in carrying out our practice. I hope all practitioners may benefit from the methods explored in this text.

Spiritual cultivation begins with three prerequisites:
- We must take both general and specific steps.
- We must use all our strengths and improve upon our weaknesses.
- We must find and cultivate diverse resources for practice.

First: What do we mean by general and specific steps?

Everything in the world is organized in terms of the General and the Specific.

A country's policies include long-term and short-term plans, as well as general and specific measures that help to achieve set goals. Any worthwhile endeavor requires us to first develop a general framework. Only after a general framework is established, can the details bring the endeavor to completion. The planning for any vision we wish to make a reality must outline the general and specific frameworks. This is true for everything.

Therefore, any plan for our Spiritual Cultivation must firmly establish a framework which is based on three principles: Spiritual

Cultivation, Cultivation of Wisdom and Inquiry, and Choice in Action. Next, the framework should be filled in to include these specific areas of mindfulness: the essential conditions of character and the important details of karmic accountability. This is the wise approach to practice.

As we outline our plan for practice, we need to further develop plans for each stage of life, each year, and each day. In this way, we develop a framework to guide us day by day throughout our lives.

Second: What is meant by using our strengths and improving upon our weaknesses?

All people have strengths and weaknesses; areas of superiority and inferiority; and aspects of robustness and frailty. The lessons from our past lives and the temperament we are born with influence the different aspects of our nature. Spiritual cultivation requires making an accurate diagnosis of where we stand right now. We must then seek appropriate measures to address our weaknesses. We must smooth our rough parts, reduce our misdeeds, and supplement shortcomings in order to sculpt ourselves into someone complete and whole. The deliberate steps we take toward Spiritual Cultivation transform our lives.

Therefore, an accurate diagnosis of one's personal reality is essential.

It is important that we discover and address our shortcomings, starting with profound reflection on our weaknesses.

Each of us also has areas of our character where we excel. Now consider what happens when our weakness is laziness. When laziness is present, all our strengths like knowledge, wisdom, and other capabilities are for naught; we cannot access them. It is crucial to address and remedy laziness through diligence. We must reflect deeply on the fact that our practice is based on diligent effort and that we need to work to correct even the slightest error in our character.

Third: We must find and cultivate diverse resources for practice.

We are often advised to maintain a balanced diet. Otherwise, we deprive ourselves of nutrients that are essential to our health. Our body requires three basic types of nutrients (proteins, carbohydrates, and fats), as well as vitamins and minerals. It is only when our nutritional needs are met that we can maintain a healthy body.

Moreover, if we are deprived of certain nutrients, we suffer a physiological imbalance which can then cause weakness and even death.

The same is true of our character. Lopsided Spiritual Cultivation that doesn't consider diversity can lead to malnutrition, leaving us with an unbalanced character. We need to seek out the diverse nutrients that our character needs.

For instance, there are some who say the only way to cultivate "The Way" is to sever all relationships and isolate yourself. This idea suggests that we need to leave sensory conditions behind. But even when we do this well, we are engaging only in Spiritual Cultivation at rest. What about our weaknesses when we are in action? Conversely, how will those who only engage in Spiritual Cultivation during action handle their weaknesses at times of rest? We must be wary of such disparities, because they leave us with an unbalanced character.

These days, there are many institutions where Spiritual Cultivation is taught. However, it is a grave mistake to focus solely on one special method of practice. As we establish our own plan for practice, we need to draw upon various methods and use them effectively. A parent with a child is called upon at times to feed her, put her to bed, play with her, get her to study, and to give the appropriate punishments and rewards. As a result, the child grows over the course of hours, days, and years into an exemplary adult.

The wise approach is to establish a practical plan for practice based on these three major principles.

Chapter 6

Our Spiritual Cultivation Plan

Whether we are talking about managing a household, a company, a group or a nation, there is a world of difference between following a well-conceived, purposeful plan or simply going with the flow of events. Unexpected developments can occur even when we have a clear plan of action, but regression will more likely occur when we lack one. Our practice is no exception.

General steps are organized around the timeline of a lifespan. Based on the characteristics of each stage of life, our focus shifts to include a period of training in scientific and religious capabilities. Then to a period of working for the world and living creatures, and finally a period of preparing for the next life. Specific plans and programs are also created for regular and daily practice to live in accordance with this annual plan, all the while making appropriate adjustments to achieve balance on a regular basis.

Specific steps are made for each day. We draft daily plans for our everyday life and specific plans to carry out based on two periods of our time: when we are busy and when we have free time.

When we do this with a willingness to make it a lifelong endeavor, we will undergo a maturation process over time. Even if we exert only minimal effort, this will naturally become our routine from day to day, an ordinary sequence that feels comfortable to us.

LIFETIME PLAN

A lifetime plan is intended to enrich all of our lives. We live countless lives, therefore we need to make plans for approaching the three major periods of our life: infancy/childhood/adolescence, middle age, and old age.

(1) Infancy, Childhood, and Adolescence

This is a period of growth in body and spirit. It is a crucial time, one where we cannot let our guard down for even a moment. We need particular attention from our parents and our community during this time.

Particularly adolescence is a time when the mind and spirit are just starting to form. Our minds expand with our efforts, so we must ensure we do not waste any of our mental and spiritual power at this time.

(2) What is childhood and adolescence planning?

Adolescence is a period when young people are beginning to develop mentally and spiritually. At this time, their minds are open, so it is best to avoid wasting unnecessary energy. Instead, they should begin to direct their mind toward a future of self-sufficiency by broadening their knowledge of the Way and science, which will allow them to gain right realization. In addition, adolescents should be supported by the guardians, parents, and teachers around them. In this sense, it is essential that those around the adolescent also form plans and guide them at the same time as they begin making plans for themselves. This will broaden their knowledge and perspective in religion and science and nurture right awareness.

The blood and energy are still unsettled, and we must guard against the attractions of beauty.

(3) Middle Age

Middle age marks the time when the concepts we learned and mastered over the course of our infancy, childhood, and adolescence have entered a period of maturation. We must therefore put what we learned to good use. Dedicating ourselves diligently to helping our home, society, country, and world. In this way the grace we have cultivated reaches far and wide. Those who spend their days idly during this time will incur a great debt to the world.

The blood and energy are growing, and we must guard against conflict.

(4) Old Age

Old age is an important period when we need to bring this life to a close and make preparations for death and our next life. We must shed the nihilistic belief that everything will be over. We need to work according to a plan as we confront the tasks of great liberation, resolve the grave matters of life and death, and prepare for our next life. Practitioners should make every effort to prepare themselves for eternal life.

Yearly Plan

A yearly plan is created for each year of our life. Within this broader framework, we divide the period up into daily practice and retreat practice, drafting separate plans for each.

(1) Retreat Practice

Retreat practice refers to a special period we set aside for leaving our everyday routine to focus solely on cultivating our practice.

When we as practitioners work, we work hard, as though we will be doing this job for a thousand or ten thousand years. Nevertheless, we must be able to step away from our work as though it never happened and approach our retreat practice with a mind that has returned to nothing. Once we arrive at the retreat, we must wholeheartedly become the practitioner: shedding all other labels, status, honors, authority, or prestige that we may have accumulated in our daily life.

The proper approach is mind practice. It is liberation and release from mental fixations and constraints, as well as escape from fearsome karmic obstacles that have tainted our minds. We are cleaning away that which pollutes our mind.

Only after the mind has been purified, can we attain the supreme enlightenment of the buddha or bodhisattva. Only after our mind is empty as the void, can it hold something of new value. As we accept this approach to the mind into our retreat practice, we should complete the following steps and processes:

First are the methods of *Spiritual Cultivation,* which focus on reciting the buddha's name and practicing sitting meditation.

In our chanting practice, we repeat the words "*Na-mu A-mi-ta Bul*" (Homage to Amitābha buddha, the buddha of Limitless Life and Light) or a designated mantra over and over until our scattered mind is centered. Practitioners practice sitting meditation by resting their mind and energy on the lower abdomen, the energy center, remaining purely in the realm of stillness and non-duality.

Generally, we recite the buddha's name when we are confronted with coarse and weighty defilements or suffering from sensory conditions. We practice sitting meditation when we're faced with minor defilements and aren't contending with sensory conditions that cause us suffering. Therefore, we should make appropriate use of each method according to our situation.

Next, there are various subjects for *Cultivation of Wisdom and Inquiry.* They are the scriptures, lectures, dharma conversations, as well as the study of the principle of our true nature, cases for inquiry, and a daily diary.

Everything related to the practice is presented to us in the scriptures. The study of them is essential for anyone who wants to engage in practice.

In lectures and dharma conversations, we share our wisdom with others or with the public. This subject allows us to work towards turning wisdom into pure gold and flawless jade.

We aim to understand our true nature through the study of the principles of our original mind, cases for inquiry, and the world of principles—great and small, and being and nonbeing.

In our mind diary, we take note of the time we've used productively and the time we've wasted. We write down the functioning of our body and mind, as well as our perceptions and impressions. Through daily reflection, we notice a natural opening of our knowledge and perspective.

The subjects for *Choice in Action* include the keeping of a daily diary, mindfulness, and conduct.

In our daily diary, we record our handling of affairs, noting whether they were mindful or unmindful. During our study, we should examine the state of our changing mind and development.

Mindfulness refers to the state of mind in which we remain watchful and cautious with our choices, remembering what we should do and should not to do in any given situation.

Conduct refers to the mind-set of disciplining ourselves with manners and actions appropriate to being a part of society, and the world at large.

(2) Daily Practice

Daily practice refers to turning every aspect of our everyday life into training. In other words, training where we practice as we work and work as we practice. Through daily practice, we carry out our life and training in tandem, bringing them together as one. This includes the actions we must do on our occasional visits to temple, as well as actions for mindfulness in daily practice.

We must be mindful of the following actions when visiting a temple or spiritual community: Engaging in questions and answers about the activities in which we have been involved; reporting our awakenings for the appraisal of a spiritual mentor; presenting matters that have raised doubts and clarifying those doubts; and preparing for our retreat practice. During regular dharma meetings, we must attend and dedicate ourselves exclusively to practice, implementing the lessons we have acquired.

The items of mindfulness in daily practice include making choices based on sound thought when encountering any sensory conditions. This involves studying and preparing things ahead of time by observing the circumstances of any given situation; studying and practicing the scriptures, ancient classics, and working on koans during free time; reciting the buddha's name and practicing sitting meditation in the morning and at night; and reflecting on our day.

Daily Plan

For our daily plan, we should develop everyday guidelines for the tasks we should be doing at any given time or place. These plans help us respond to the circumstances we encounter in daily life.

(1) Everyday Plan

Our everyday plan outlines how we will develop our powers of attention when we have work to attend to as well as our powers of concentration when we do not.

When we have work to attend to, we should strive to make sound choices in all our obligations. In doing so, we ensure that our work proceeds well, while we develop our powers of attention and one pointed mind. Thus, we should follow a three-stage process when handling our affairs.

When sensory conditions arise, whether favorable or unfavorable, we should:

1) Stop and recover soundness of mind
2) Apply our thoughts based on a sound mind to attain proper judgment
3) Choose the right and abandon the wrong based on solid judgment

As we repeat the above steps in our encounters with sensory conditions, our powers of one pointed mind and attention will develop, our work will proceed successfully, and our capabilities will grow to an unlimited extent. If we persist in this effort, we will attain the ability to easily handle any and every task we are given. What a marvelous method this is!

When we are at rest with no work to attend to, we should remove all defilements and develop our mental powers of concentration through recitation of the buddha's name, sitting meditation, prayer, reading of the scriptures, and study. In doing so, we recover our original mind and refresh ourselves with calm energy. If we persist in this effort, we will attain the power of meditation and gain control of our consciousness. With this as the result, what could be a better practice?

We must face every step of this process with a mind that strives to accumulate merit, wasting no time or spiritual energy, so that with the passage of time and our dedication, we eventually will reach the stage of freedom.

(2) Daily Routine

Our daily routine outlines the course of our day, which we must follow fully with one mind.

Mornings are dedicated to Spiritual Cultivation and Cultivation of Wisdom and Inquiry.

Midday is dedicated to requital of gratitude and service to the public.

Night time is dedicated to reflection, repentance, and spiritual cultivation.

A mind of tremendous diligence and discipline is needed if we hope to adhere to this demanding routine. We will never succeed if we are lazy. In fact, no one has ever accomplished great things, who has lived a scattered life without principles. All successful people have integrated their principles with absolute completeness and lived lives of diligence.

Here is a more specific explanation of this daily routine.

Our daily routine starts when we rise at 4:30 or 5:00 in the morning. We set our alarm clock to ensure that we do not sleep past this time. We do not mindlessly leap out of bed the moment we awake. Instead, we relax our stiff bodies and rise with a mind of gratitude as we greet a new day of hope. We make our bed and wash up, and then we follow this with a prayer of gratitude, a vow, and a pledge.

Next, we proceed to a routine of sitting meditation; reading and reciting scriptures; studying cases for inquiry; cleaning; eating breakfast; doing our work; eating lunch; continuing our work; having dinner; taking care of any remaining task; showering; writing in our daily diary to reflect on our day; reading the scriptures or performing spiritual cultivation; at last doing our nightly prayer at 9:30 and going to bed.

It is essential that we proceed with one pointed mind during each step along our way. Otherwise, we merely go through the motions and risk becoming enthralled in all sorts of defilements and idle thoughts, dredging up past matters, or thinking of things that have yet to come. When this happens, our efforts are diminished. For instance, even when we experience the state of flow at any given moment, we must be able to stop at the sound of the evening bell and concentrate on our prayer. In cases where we are engaged in silent prayer outwardly while enmeshed in past thoughts or idle thoughts within our mind, our prayer will not be effective. We must boldly release any thoughts or obstacles and push ahead toward our goal.

We will reap great rewards simply by adhering to our routine, performing each step with one pointed mind. We must approach every daily routine with great determination to not let go of one pointed mind at any point. We must not release our one pointed mind, even for a moment.

With each practice our one pointed mind is developed. Our powers of one pointed mind grow from moment to moment until they eventually manifest as an awesome force. As our depth of spiritual cultivation increases, our work succeeds. Indescribable good fortune and blessings accumulate.

These diverse measures offer us the perfect opportunity to enter the genuine realm of the stillness and non-duality of our true nature. All practitioners should exert themselves in practice each step of the way.

When our daily routine is alive,
The life force of right dharma is alive,
And the life force of our individual character as a practitioner of the Way is vibrant.

When our daily routine collapses,
So do the fundamentals of right dharma,
And the fundamentals of our character as practitioner collapse.

CHAPTER 7

Our Vow and Repentance

No discussion of practice would be complete without mentioning vows and repentance. Practitioners work endlessly to address and strengthen these commitments. If our vow to attain great enlightenment for the benefit of all sentient beings is weak, then all the knowledge we have gained will ultimately become useless and will create no meaningful consequence. A weak commitment to repentance means we cannot purify our karma or truly move forward on the path.

If our vow is a limitless motivating force, then repentance is a light to shine upon our path. Without this motivating force and light, the process of cultivating the Way will be very slow and, in fact, may never be fully realized. Our vow is like the reins guiding us forward, while repentance is like the whip that spurs us on from behind. When the practitioner's mind is driven by right encouragement and right guidance, there will be no room for disbelief, greed, laziness, or ignorance to enter into it.

Won-Buddhism instructs us to offer our vow in prayer in the morning, and to offer our reflection and repentance in prayer at night, both as part of our committed daily practice. We are also asked to offer our vow and additional prayers at the beginning and end of each month, as we reflect and repent.

We begin and end the year with this practice as well. As we can see, vows and repentance are a fundamental aspect of Won-Buddhism.

Additionally, as part of our daily practice, we recite the Il-Won-Sang Vow every morning and we set aside time for silent reading of scriptures and other spiritual teachings.

If we perform each of these actions with utmost dedication and sincerity, many obstacles along our path will be removed.

The ultimate goal of our vow is to attain the great power of universal truth and to be united with its nature. The ultimate goal of repentance is to abolish every single speck of the dust of deception that remains inside or outside our minds and hearts.

Won-Buddhism directs us to make a vow to seek buddhahood and to deliver all sentient beings from their suffering. As discussed below, we are also directed to perform both Repentance in Principle and Repentance in Action. Attaining buddhahood means achieving perfection within ourselves. Delivering sentient beings refers to the altruism of the Mahayana practice.

Repentance in Action is a practice that addresses our individual transgressive actions. When we transgress, we ask forgiveness and make Buddha offerings directly to every person affected by that transgression, as well as to the Three Jewels, namely, the Buddha, the Dharma, and the Sangha. Repentance in Principle is a practice that addresses the whole of our transgressions and our tendency to transgress. When we practice Repentance in Principle, we dissolve our transgressions by awakening to our true nature which is inherently devoid of transgressions.

We cannot hope to clear away our old transgressive karma without engaging in these practices. Neglecting these practices could sweep us into former and future karma without a means for escape. Great zeal and courage are absolutely essential.

For this reason, we must never stop practicing both, our great vow and repentance.

CHAPTER 8

MINDFULNESS AND ONE POINTED MIND

When practicing meditation, we must commit with sincere dedication to reciting the buddha's name and to sitting meditation during times of rest. However, during times of action, we need to be attentive to one pointed mind in everything we do.

One pointed mind refers to our mindfulness in eliminating the wrong and proceeding with the right. Right and wrong exist for all things. From our minds to our actions, and from our actions to our minds, right and wrong are always present. Mindfulness, and one pointed mind, develops when we devote ourselves to focusing solely on the heedful mind that chooses right over wrong. If mindfulness represents the beginning, then one pointed mind is the result.

If we continue cultivating this One Mind, we will someday reach the stage of great samadhi, where we can maintain a perfect, still and meditative state of mind. This is also called samadhi in Action, a meditation dharma through which we can engage in spiritual cultivation whenever and with whatever we are experiencing. Samadhi in Action is a method in which we never leave the meditative state of mind, not even for a brief moment. The merits of this way of meditation allow for the possibility of simultaneous practice of universal principles and human affairs, as well as wholeness of both spirit and body. Through Samadhi in Action, we will realize that buddhadharma is daily life and daily life is buddhadharma.

Yet many practitioners underestimate the immense value of having one pointed mind in each and every daily affair, so they make no effort at all to achieve this power. They cannot let go of their fixation on the idea that practice should only consist of sitting meditation. This is terribly foolish and disappointing. Such individuals fail to understand the principle of the mind. This fixation is what prompts the warning, "this is sickly meditation." If we can only practice while seated and not when standing, working, walking, etc., then we are in trouble.

The mind has the ability to develop as it is disciplined. Those who discipline themselves with one pointed mind while driving will enhance their driving skills. Those who discipline themselves with one pointed mind while performing music will enhance their musical skills. Those who discipline themselves with one pointed mind when practicing calligraphy will develop those abilities and see their skill improve day by day. Those who develop one pointed mind in reading will develop reading capabilities and acquire vast stores of knowledge. And that is not all! When we develop one pointedness of mind in each and every situation, these innumerable forms of concentration will combine so we can develop new capabilities that allow us to aptly perform anything and everything.

If we fail to develop one pointed mind, we will not be able to realize our full capabilities. We may also find that success only comes from what interests us which will ultimately restrict us from realizing the full breath of what life has to offer.

As we continue to cultivate a one pointed mind in each and every action, attachments will disappear, delusive thoughts will be extinguished, and our mind will be completely cleansed. As a result, our understanding of human affairs and universal principles will grow. At the same time, we will develop and grow practical decision-making abilities based on the dharma, no matter what sensory conditions surround us.

"The Dharma of Timeless Meditation" in *The Principal Book of*

Won-Buddhism it is said that those who practice meditation over a long period of time "will be centered like an iron pillar and stand strong like a stone wall." "Practicing all dharmas in this way," you will never be distracted or obstructed. You will attain hundreds and thousands of samadhis, even while residing in this secular world. And you will reach a gateway to freedom from birth and death—liberation from the cycle of rebirths.

Therefore, the practitioner who disciplines themselves internally through the recitation of the buddha's name and by sitting meditation while at rest, and also develops the pointed mind in each and every action, can achieve a limitless expansion of his meditation powers, as action and rest become one single and continuous state of mind.

We need to make ample use of the power we gain from meditation, both in our daily lives, and in the practice of cultivating wisdom, so we can eventually attain great enlightenment. Spiritual Cultivation, which is an essential aspect of the Threefold Practice is also the foundation of Mindful Choice in Action as well as the Middle Path. An effective method of practice that anyone can do, it improves and enriches both our spiritual path and our everyday lives.

Mindfulness practice is an effective method to lead humankind from the sea of suffering into paradise. As our civilization develops and the world becomes more complex, the more essential and indispensable this practice becomes.

Of the many disasters that have befallen humankind in recent years, there is not one that did not occur from a lack of mindfulness. Yet we see almost no effort being made to find and fix this deficiency in our minds.

The greater our dreams, the more we require the abilities we gain through mindfulness practice. All matters, whether personal or public, become clear when mindfulness guides us. Mindfulness practice helps accomplish our greatest dreams and realizations during our lifetimes.

Great things can happen when the scope of mindfulness is broad; only small things happen when that scope is narrow.

For this reason, to succeed in anything, we need to develop mindfulness—starting small and working our way up.

When mindfulness extends into the smallest aspects of our behavior, the chances of success will increase accordingly, without perceived extra effort on our part.

We will always achieve less when we neglect our mindfulness practice, and we may, instead, end up submerged in a sea of suffering. We need to create a practice of mindfulness. There is a great difference between what we intend in theory and what we do in reality. Mindfulness practice needs to become a habit—it needs to be a constant in our lives. Then it will breach the difference between what we can achieve with partial effort and what we can do with great dedication and zeal.

For mindful actions and unmindful actions alike, the results come back to us eventually. They return in different forms according to the nature of the issues involved. Sometimes, they come quickly. Other times, slowly. Sometimes, we recognize the results. At other times, we don't. Sometimes, we need to repeat the mindfulness or unmindfulness over and over, until it reaches a critical point, before the results comes back to us. Other times, they all come at once. In some cases, like traffic accidents, we may have shown mindfulness ninety-nine times, yet ended up with a devastating outcome because of one single instance of unmindfulness. There are also cases where the results may come directly or indirectly. Indeed, in some instances, they may be indirect by several degrees of separation—two, three, four, five, or more. In every case, the consequences of our mindfulness or unmindfulness come back to us to produce good fortune or misfortune.

When we reach the state of complete and consistent mindfulness practice, we will eventually achieve the restoration of our true nature. Only when we reach this stage, do the great powers of liberation and freedom of mind arise.

Therefore, we must carry on with thorough mindfulness practice according to the practice methods of mindfulness. Let us examine and understand the various types of mindfulness to help determine the right path.

Inconsistent versus Consistent Mindfulness

When we engage in Inconsistent Mindfulness, our heedfulness is determined by sensory conditions and our mood is unstable. In Consistent Mindfulness, we set standards and extend our heedfulness consistently as a form of practice.

Everyday Mindfulness and Visionary Mindfulness

With everyday mindfulness, we are heedful only as the need arises in our daily life. In visionary mindfulness, we extend heedfulness for the purpose of realizing a vision at all times.

Temporary versus Long-Term Mindfulness

With temporary mindfulness, we are heedful only on an impromptu and momentary basis and only under special circumstances. Long-term mindfulness means extending heedfulness consistently and continuously in accordance with our goal.

Simple versus Complex Mindfulness

Simple mindfulness is being attentive only when matters interest us. Complex mindfulness means being attentive as we attend to many different matters including those of lesser or even of no particular interest to us.

Individual and Collective Mindfulness

Individual mindfulness means being heedful only of matters concerning ourselves. With collective mindfulness, all members of a group commit to a single mind based on a common goal.

Superficial and Profound Mindfulness

With superficial mindfulness, we are heedful only of superficial matters. Profound mindfulness means demonstrating heedfulness as we delve into a world of profundity and mystery.

It is important to closely examine the kind of mindfulness we are engaged in. As we maintain our mindfulness practice through trying and calm situations, we gradually develop the meditative power of the one pointed mind. We will then face no constraints or obstructions and we will be resourceful in any situation we encounter. Eventually we arrive at the stage of single-practice samadhi and single-image samadhi, and we will open gateways to unlimited blessings and wisdom for ourselves and others.

The Nature of Mindfulness:

1. Living with an awakened mind: Understanding the activity of our mind and body (the six sense organs) and the phenomena we encounter from the outside. (the six sensory conditions)
2. Living assiduously: Determining and proceeding with perseverance in everything we do in our life, our practice, and maintaining our moral compass.
3. Living cautiously: Responding appropriately to the various dangers such as survival, practice, and conduct that we face while making our way through the inevitable turbulence of life.
4. Living a goal-oriented life: Having the mind-set to establish and pursue wholesome goals in everything we do.
5. Living wisely: Efficiently using our knowledge as we observe human affairs and universal principles

The Directions of Mindfulness:

1. Goal Orientation: At the heart of mindfulness, there must be an orientation toward the achievement of wholesome goals
2. Completeness: When we are mindful, we must examine all aspects of our aims and goals.
3. Exactitude: The essence of mindfulness practice must be

scrupulously observed in detail.

4. Timeliness: Our mindfulness should be appropriately timed to the type of situation we are facing.

5. Ambition: Our mindfulness must conform to the requirements of a grand vision for the goal of all.

6. Efficiency: Our mindfulness should be efficient and produce good results in all the areas listed above.

CHAPTER 9

Obstacles to Spiritual Cultivation

It is clear that cultivation and practice are absolutely required and urgently needed in the world. People can be deterred from attempting true spiritual cultivation and practice by many things. Anyone who walks this path will see obstacles arise in practice. Seemingly, these obstacles may never go away or improve. Sometimes, they even cajole us. Other times, they threaten us. They may test us with enticement and seduction. The deeper we get into our study, the more tests and obstructions of Mara we will encounter. As practitioners, we must treat these obstacles as teachers, learning from them and allowing them to fuel our devotion to our practice.

We need to develop the discernment to identify which of Mara's obstructions may appear in the path of our practice to immediately detect and boldly remove them when they occur. The most crucial hindrances are those of *disbelief*, *greed*, *laziness*, and *ignorance*. We cannot allow these to stand in the way of our practice. Once they have established themselves, we may never enter the Way during this lifetime. These hindrances can make any spiritual cultivation or practice utterly impossible.

Disbelief is when we do not believe in the truth, the proper dharma instructions, and the right teachers and colleagues. It prevents us from reaching good decisions when conducting our affairs.

Greed is when we desire too much of something, becoming fixated on unhealthy desires. With this mind, we reach for too much of everything, straying from the Way which can only lead to negative results.

Laziness is lacking the desire to exert ourselves. When we are lazy, we lose the will for activity and avoid work when attempting to conduct our affairs. No one can move forward along the Way with such a mindset.

Ignorance is a lack of knowledge. A greater ignorance still is when we ignore circumstances, yet do not seek to understand them. A more firmly entrenched ignorance is found in those who are ignorant of their own ignorance. When we fail to understand the principles of great and small, being and nonbeing, and affairs of right and wrong, gain and loss, we end up doing only what pleases us, racing finally toward unrelenting self-indulgence.

It is extremely difficult to practice once any of these mindsets are in place.

We must absolutely abandon these four hindrances when we engage in practice.

There are several other minds besides these which prevent us from readily pursuing spiritual cultivation and practice:
- the mind which has succumbed to inertia
- the mind hampered by the notion that practice is a mountain that is impossible to climb or a barrier that is too high to scale
- the mind solely interested in worldly matters
- the mind locked into unhealthy habits
- the mind trapped in an impenetrable self-made cave of isolation
- the mind unfocused and unable to withstand external conditions

The mind succumbed to inertia is settled deeply into a basic routine from which it cannot escape. It has no greater goals than meeting the needs of clothing, food, and shelter. It lacks aspiration or hope and adopts a complacent attitude toward most situations that arise. With this mind, we abandon all hope of improvement and are unable to show any exertion or zeal. We merely exist half-heartedly and thus the vitality of our mind withers.

The mind that views practice as an unscalable cliff becomes fearful, viewing practice as an impossible task even before making an attempt. With this mindset we have given up on trying to do things because of a mind that dismisses our own spiritual capacity and a foolish belief that such a thing is utterly beyond us. We cannot make even one step toward progress with this way of thinking. No matter what words of persuasion we hear, we cannot escape our own thoughts. We cannot make the slightest step toward practice without shedding these stubborn thoughts.

The mind that dwells on the notion of an impassable barrier is habituated to merely listening without exploring, thinking we have heard it all before. In such cases, we are trapped by a notion that we already know the dharma or we have learned all there is to learn. We make no effort to put those instructions into practice. With such a mindset we may understand things through the wisdom of discrimination, but we can never enter the true realm of practice.

Our mind, interested only in worldly things, has all its thoughts focused on the affairs of the world, showing no interest and no need to look within. It is filled completely with mundane matters. With such a mind, we cannot enter the world of endless marvels.

The mind made up of rigid habits becomes chain binding and prevents us from escaping the practices we developed in previous lives. All of us are bound to have such habits, but in this case the improper habits have settled so deeply that they've become stifling. They become extraordinarily difficult to escape—indeed, we may only succeed in doing so if we make the fullest use of self-reliance *and* allow ourselves to rely on others. When bad habits have such control over us, it is a challenge to escape and embark on the path to practice. Seeking the support of others can be a great blessing.

When we speak of the mind trapped in an impenetrable cave, we are referring to a life of being confined inwardly. It is as though a cavern has been excavated in our mind and fortified so that no one can see inside; even we ourselves cannot see outside of it. All manner of afflictions and ills may come and we can do nothing about them. We can only understand the state of the world if we break free, but we continue to live with the door tightly shut. Unless we escape from this mind, we can never enter the Gateway of Practice and proceed toward freedom.

When we talk of the mind consumed by external conditions, we are speaking of a mind that merely follows along with the conditions of the real world's right and wrong, gain and loss, its conditions of joy, anger, sadness, and pleasure—its favorable and adverse conditions. In other words, our soul is held captive by every sensory condition we encounter. We fail to perceive this trap and therefore have no thought of escape. As a result, we are incapable of producing the mind that pursues spiritual cultivation and practice.

Beyond those hindrances, we may view work and spiritual cultivation as conflicting concepts. We fixate on the idea that we cannot engage in spiritual cultivation when we are working and that we must refrain from working if we wish to cultivate ourselves. We hesitate, balk, and lose precious time. We hesitate, thinking we will get around to it after we've accomplished our work—but we never actually do. When we acquire the idea of cultivating as we work and working as we cultivate, and understand that *all things* are resources for practice, only then will we arrive in the realm of true practice. If we look at work and cultivation as conflicting, we are unlikely to ever reach that place of peace.

There is also the procrastinating mind, which says, "I'll do it tomorrow." Such a mind prevents us from reaching the realm of spiritual cultivation. There is no end of tomorrows; there will never be a day when the procrastinating mind comes to a halt. It is difficult indeed for us to ever reach the realm of true spiritual cultivation with such a mind.

All the hindrances described here are the minions of Mara preventing us from reaching the true realm of spiritual cultivation and practice. Only when we boldly and courageously overcome them may we enter the gateway of spiritual cultivation and practice.

CHAPTER 10

DIARY FOR SPIRITUAL PRACTICE

So far, I have tried to arouse interest in the reader by providing a clear understanding of the true nature of the mind. I have also sought to use that understanding as a basis for exploring the type of care and the kind of practice the mind requires, and to set a path for its cultivation.

To this end, I outlined clear and practical steps we can take to cultivate our mind. They are more than ideas or concepts. I have described several methods for entering and practicing within the true realm of spiritual cultivation so we can prevent various forms of regression.

The dharma of Keeping a Diary is significant as a immediate means of preventing regression in our spiritual cultivation practice.

If we do not apply a concrete method, we may find a crack in our resolution to cultivate the mind, and before we know it, all our efforts might end in dissolution.

As is the case with everything in this world, it is essential that we choose the most rational and efficient path to achieve our goal, directing our movement forward continuously without allowing it to be thwarted by welcome or unwelcome occurrences that may arise. If we are to do this, it is both essential and wise to take specific steps as we travel down our chosen path. This is all the more important when it comes to our practice.

There is no end to the obstructions that Mara and its minions impart to our practice, and their incursions are stealthy indeed. If we are not alert to them, we will find ourselves overcome by them before we are even aware it is happening. If this occurs, we may engage with them as though they were our friends.

Worse still, we may come to regard them as our masters and allow ourselves to become their obedient slaves, doing their bidding without hesitation, and engaging in situations in which we would never otherwise participate. We must never allow these dark forces to gain entrance into our minds by means of practicing what we call "the dharma of the gateway of our original nature." Once Mara has infiltrated us, we need to have the mental strength and courage to battle and overcome it. It is far better to abide in our true nature that is originally empty, guarding it fully, so nothing can invade it or disrupt its fundamental capacity for loving-kindness.

This requires rigorous effort at each step of the way.

We need to establish what works and what doesn't, and we need to determine when a situation is working well or is beginning to go astray. Acquiring the capacity to determine what has the potential to become successful or unsuccessful provides a method of practice that we can use as medicine every time sensory stimuli arise. This is the dharma of self-assessment—we keep a diary in which we examine ourselves.

Won-Buddhism sets the direction of the Cultivation of our minds by means of the Threefold Practice, the Eight Articles, the Fourfold Grace, the Essential Discourse of Commanding Our Nature, and the Precepts. These practices are blueprints for what to do and what not to do. Won-Buddhism also provides us with the Essential Dharmas of Daily Practice, which enable us to get to the heart of our practice and facilitate the forward motion of our path. Then, it provides us with the Dharma of Keeping a Diary for self-assessment, to help us avoid any possible regression. These different Dharmas lead us on the path of a complete practice

There are two types of diaries in the dharma of Keeping a Diary—a Mind Diary, which we mainly use for self-assessment and recording of events especially during retreat, and a Daily Mindfulness Journal that we use in our daily practice. Let us look briefly at the methods of self-assessment and recording used in each one of them.

Keeping A Daily Mindfulness Journal

A. Examining and recording the number of times we were mindful or unmindful
Mindful: The mind of choosing action with sound thought
Unmindful: The mind of not choosing action with sound thought

① We may select certain things to do or not to do.
② We may follow things to do or not to do according to the doctrine.
③ We may examine and record all areas of practice.
④ It is mindfulness if we had a heedful mind from the beginning, and unmindfulness if we did not. It is mindfulness if it ultimately succeeds, and unmindfulness if it does not.

B. Recording the Assessment of our studies
① Recording the timing of our cultivation practice
② Recording the timing of our inquiry practice
③ Recording whether we attended dharma meetings
④ IRecording the number of our transgressions of the precepts

Keeping A Mind Diary

① Record the number of hours spent practicing or wasting our

time that day
② Record the balance of our income and expenditures that day
③Record the instances of handling the function of our mind and body
④ Relating our perceptions and impressions

The Dharma of Keeping a Daily Mindfulness Journal

(1) Recording Mindfulness and Unmindfulness

In the preceding section, I gave specific information about mindfulness and unmindfulness, so I will not repeat it here. Nonetheless, I should stress that nothing in human affairs succeeds without mindfulness. Our mindfulness comes into being according to how and where we direct our minds. All things are achieved through mindfulness practice—from small to great, from practical matters to the realization of great enlightenment.

We must therefore practice mindfulness, disciplining ourselves and developing our capabilities. When our mindfulness abilities are faulty, all our worldly affairs are faulty as well. When our mindfulness abilities are perfected, so too are our worldly affairs. What we are observing and recording is the presence or the absence of heedfulness while engaged in activities we should do, and activities we should not do, in order to train ourselves in mindfulness capabilities. We are examining whether we were mindful or unmindful in every situation and when faced with every sensory condition, and adding it all up to assess our practice.

At first, we record the presence or absence of heedfulness. Then, we record events as mindful when they are successful or unmindful when they go wrong.

We then record daily, monthly, and yearly figures, to determine variables and establish forward-moving steps to bring our mindfulness capabilities into maturity.

(2) Recording the Assessment of Our Studies

Studies refers to learning and mastery. There are innumerable areas of knowledge that we must learn and master on our way to achieving our practice goals. Keeping a diary is an effective way to examine how much consideration we gave to the process of learning and mastering them.

I have explained that time we dedicate to our studies and the sensory conditions we are confronted with are the resources that fuel the forward motion of our practice. If our recording of mindfulness and unmindfulness is a way of examining our reactions to sensory conditions, then the recording of the assessment of our study is a way of evaluating the time we dedicate to them. We also need to detect and reduce the amount of time we waste.

A. Recording the Timing of Our Spiritual Cultivation (Reciting the Buddha's Name, Meditation, Prayer)

Our time spent reciting the buddha's name, practicing sitting meditation, and offering prayer, is used to develop our concentration abilities in order to achieve a tranquil, clear mind and return to the realm of our original nature.

It is said that disciplining our mind by reciting the buddha's name is like using coarse sandpaper, whereas practicing sitting meditation is like using fine sandpaper. Together, these three practices: chanting, meditation and prayer are essential elements of spiritual cultivation through which we nurture our mind and replenish our spirit.

What we need to examine here is how much time we have dedicated to them. The time that we spend concentrating with One Mind on these three things is truly crucial in our practice. The very fact that we can have such occasions is an invaluable treasure and good fortune. The person who genuinely knows this value and merit has already reached the stage of sainthood.

B. Recording Our Inquiry Times (Scriptures, Dharma Talks, Dharma Conversations, The Principle of Our Nature, Studying Cases for Questioning)

The inquiry into the scriptures, dharma talks, dharma conversations, studying the principle of our nature, and koan study help us to cultivate our wisdom in many respects. Today, we see people who aspire to awakening, yet do nothing but wait for a sudden epiphany to come upon them one day. This is not a reasonable expectation. There may be some people who possess a high spiritual capacity based on engaging in a lot of cultivation in past lives. They may have a spiritual capacity of innate knowledge. However, even then, they experience enlightenment only as the result of having accumulated merit over the course of many lives. They did not always possess the spiritual capacity for sudden enlightenment and sudden cultivation.

The reason that we are asked to train ourselves with these

practices, together or separately, is to cultivate wisdom from various angles, depending on our situations. Those who carry out this process diligently will eventually attain hundreds or thousands of realizations, that will lead to attaining great enlightenment.

This is a superb, efficient, and sure method that anyone is capable of. However, there is an essential requirement: we must face each step along the way with sincere dedication and diligence. In our diary, we examine and record the number of hours that we spent considering our inquiry process.

C. Recording Our Attendance to Dharma Meetings

Attendance at dharma meetings is meaningful in several regards. Let us look at what is gained from dropping everything that we are doing without regret and attending service.

Dharma meetings develop our power to boldly leave behind the "real-life" issues that we unwittingly find ourselves fixating on. They allow us escape from the inertia that limits us to our routine. They provide an occasion for refreshing the spirit of faith and an opportunity to encounter the spirits of sages. Dharma meetings offer an opportunity to meet with the sages and teachers of our time. They let us reclaim our humility by dropping the arrogance that we unwittingly accumulate. Dharma meetings help us create strong dharma ties with our fellow practitioners in eternal life. This allows us to learn from ourselves and from each other and experience the grace of learning. As a result, the world becomes a clearer, brighter, and warmer place, opening the gateway for achieving enlightenment for ourselves and others.

There are those who think that attending dharma meetings is something for fools or those of low spiritual capacity. It is shallow and thoughtless to underrate the importance of attendance because of our own concept of our high spiritual capacity. Therefore, to disregard visits or dispute their importance is a foolish approach that blocks the way to progression.

Thus, we are instructed to examine our visits and record them in our diary, which protects us from a lazy mind.

D. Recording Our Transgressions of the Precepts

The precepts constitute alert mindfulness; a warning stemming from great loving-kindness and compassion from the sages, who seek to rescue ordinary humans and sentient beings from the danger of falling onto an immoral path and facing innumerable torments. Considering this goal, how could we fail to pay attention to them? Rather, we must strive diligently to avoid transgression, and to remove any transgression we have already acquired. We are instructed to address and observe each and every precept. In so doing, we are examining the changes in ourselves, confirming them, and responding appropriately.

The Dharma of Keeping a Mind Diary

In our daily diary, we examine and record things regardless of whether it is a retreat practice period or not. During those training periods, we also keep a mind diary with content as follows.

A. Recording the Day's Work and Wasted Time

Working time refers to when we engage in meaningful, necessary, and productive effort. This contrasts with wasted time, which is spent on things that are not meaningful, necessary, or productive. As a result, time working is when we create blessings and build our capabilities, while time wasted is when we incur debts and allow our capabilities to wither.

B. Recording the Day's Balance of Income and Expenditures

This item is intended to establish a complete sense of our finances. Finances are an inextricable element of our physical life and the basis for our clothing, food, and shelter.

Therefore, this dharma practice is not solely limited to the realm of the spiritual. Extending it to the economic domain, we are committing all our energies to the overarching principle of wholeness of both spirit and flesh.

Our responsibility is therefore to compare our daily income and expenditures and check the balance. In the process, we are acquiring a sense for reducing our expenditures when our income drops and attempting to increase our income when our expenditures demand it. This is a fundamental and essential matter for our physical and economic life, and we must strive to acquire this sense of reasoning completely through this dharma.

C. Relating Our Handling of the Mind and Body's Functioning

At all times except when we are sleeping, we are constantly using our body and mind.

We use them continuously according to what is happening, and we are constantly making choices about our action in the process. We therefore need to make a detailed account of how we used them at critical moments—what we chose and what we rejected, being wholly aware of what choices we made in our actions. Then we should have this account evaluated, while engaging in continued self-appraisal, transforming functioning of mind and body into functioning that is right, profound, and working toward the achievement of great things.

D. Relating Our Perceptions and Impressions

The word, perceptions, here does not refer to the sensory input taken in by our peripheral nerves, rather, it refers to all instances of awakening, both large and small. It refers to realization and understanding as our wisdom opens to things that we were unaware of or uninterested in before. The word, impressions, in turn, refers primarily to what we imagine based on our feelings. The maturity of our perceptions and impressions varies depending on the breadth, depth, and height of our world of thought. This is therefore a process of receiving teaching and gaining awakening from all the things we see, hear, and experience through cultivation and honing of wisdom in our perceptions and impressions.

Rather than simply overlooking our perceptions and impressions, we need to relay them to our teachers to receive appraisal, thus allowing an assessment of the changes taking place as our knowledge and perspective capacity develops. This, in turn, brings forth an awakening to every step and everything as a great sacred scripture.

In the above, I have explained about practical matters of practice, including the dharma of diary keeping. The explanation may be very general, but I tried to include all significant aspects. However, as practitioners, we must be mindful of the need to engrave these precepts upon our heart as matters of great importance, and to carry them with us in our daily practice.

Each and every dharma stage has its own distinctive meaning. When we engage in practice that combines all of them, this whole practice will lead to great results: twice the results for half the work. Good results are sure to come quickly.

There are areas of practice that I have not discussed here, yet they are all revealed to us over the course of the actions described so far, so we should be able to find a way to resolve them.

However, when we engage in one-sided practice, willfully choosing practices based on our preferences, the whole of our practice will not only be lopsided but will also generate tremendous losses both in time and in benefits, and perfection will end up beyond our reach.

All the dharma practices described above are comprehensive, sequential, and whole methods. When we follow them to the letter, we will develop a character that is perfect and complete in all respects, and we will gain great capabilities that reach anywhere and everywhere. Yet, when we take a dim view of this dharma and insist on some other special form of practice, the result, no matter how well we do, will be lopsided, and we will never be free of a fragmented character.

There is a Buddhist teaching that figuratively expresses the weakness of the fragmented character that results from lopsided practice: a buddha of mud cannot cross the water, a buddha of wood cannot cross the fire, and a buddha of metal cannot cross the furnace. In other words, the buddha of mud disintegrates when it encounters water, the buddha of wood disintegrates when it encounters fire, and the buddha of metal is unable to bear the heat and disintegrates when it enters a furnace. But the true buddha that has practiced in all directions can endure all things. This means that the results of our practice in all directions will never buckle under any circumstances.

The different dharmas of practice described above may seem like a burden, but this is the thinking of one who has not truly understood the profound meaning of what spiritual practice is. When we understand the nature and the significance of our practice, we will see that the essential dharmas in every one of their steps are effective, complete, and certain beyond the slightest shred of doubt.

In the process of practicing all of these things, the Won-Buddhism dharma practice guarantees results by preventing lopsidedness or dissipation in our practice.

When we perform each of these tasks in our retreat and daily practice, using every sensory condition and moment as a chance for practice both when we are working and when we have no work to do, the merits from this not only hold up in all circumstances, but may eventually create pure gold and flawless jade. This is what we call "Mahayana practice," the dharma of perennial practice, and the ultimate practice.

Even as we carry out the practices described above; we find situations where we achieve development with ease in some areas but none in others. All this results from learning in the past, now appearing in the present. We should not think it strange. We should instead, use every circumstance as an opportunity to strengthen our practice with great zeal. This means that we need the ability to make use of our strengths, while focusing our accumulation of merit on working constantly to address our weaknesses. We need to target these until mindfulness becomes a natural and effortless state of mind. In other words, the less successful something is, the more energy we need to put into our zeal, with a steadfast determination to see it through to the end.

Listen, listen, listen until you hear without listening.
Look, look, look until you see without looking.
Know, know, know until you understand without knowledge.
Do, do, do, until it happens by itself.

CHAPTER 11

The Stages of Mind Practice

Plants and animals go through many stages of growth. During this process, it is essential that all the right conditions are met for healthy development. If they are not, it is impossible for even a single shoot to emerge from the soil. Just as unfavorable conditions will inhibit growth, favorable conditions result in abundant growth and excellent development.

The growth of our mind is also determined by the effort we put forth in taking care of our mind. Practice is none other than taking good care of our mind, which will bring great merit. This is not a vague notion of dedication, instead, it is a specific method of exerting ourselves and accumulating merit through our commitment to carry out the steps of practice required in order to be able to articulate a rational point of view.

Pay attention to the word "rational" here. The rational point of view conforms to a fundamental truth; the irrational defies it. For example, it is rational to use grains of rice to make a bowl of rice, while is irrational to try to make a bowl of rice out of sand. Sand will never be rice, no matter how much sincerity and dedication we apply to making it so. When our point of view is rational, our efforts bring success; when it is irrational, no amount of effort can bring success.

There is no escaping this principle in our practice. Practice includes both the rational and the irrational, and it is essential that we can clearly distinguish between the two.

The growth of our practice is determined by how fully we commit ourselves to these methods. Just as the development of a butterfly passes through the phases of egg, caterpillar, cocoon, and adult, so too our spiritual transformation to attain buddhahood must undergo various phases.

If we want to move forward in our development, it is critical that we understand that each phase of mind practice will offer unique challenges we must face. Let us look at each stage, so we can recognize the milestones we will find along the way, the obstacles we are likely to face, and the skills required to overcome them. We have set ourselves to the task of taming the functioning of our six sense organs and modifying our behavior according to the dharma. What are the phases we can expect to pass through?

When we first begin our practice, our past habits constantly confront us. Our mind wants to practice, but ingrained thought patterns sidetrack us over and over again. This is completely normal, especially for the beginning practitioner. If we sharpen our ability to recognize the habitual mind, as it arises, and set it aside each time, we can free our mind from ingrained thinking and practice more mindfully. As we free ourselves from habitual patterns of thought, we may begin to notice that defilements and idle thoughts thrive in our mind. They are nothing new to us. They are the same minions of Mara that have always distracted and disturbed our spirit. We have allowed to live with them because we did not know any better. Now that we can see clearly into our mind, we recognize them for what they are. In this way, the great task of calming those defilements and unifying the distracted spirit presents itself. This is a critical phase for every practitioner.

At this stage we have broken free of the habitual mind and calmed our disturbed spirit. Next, we are faced with our desires: those things we desperately want to possess or want to do, or those that we desperately want to avoid. If we allow our desires to dictate our behavior, we will never move beyond the realm of desire. Our task is to refrain from activities we may want to do, and to do activities we may want to avoid. This is an exceptionally tall order. Turning away from our desires does not come easily or naturally and will require significant effort for most practitioners. This should be a matter of great care.

Once we have passed these milestones, a final challenge remains. We must move beyond the fence of the dharma. Our behavior may have been tamed fully by the dharma, but now the dharma itself binds us. This is perfectly understandable. The dharma provided the peace, wisdom, and strength required to get as far as we have. We depend on it and are reluctant to set it aside. Nevertheless, we need the courage to kick away the fence. This is something that is almost inhumanly difficult, yet we can only walk in the vastness of the world once we have kicked away this fence.

Once we have cleared these obstacles, they will seem trivial, in hindsight, nothing special really. But while we are in the process of confronting them, they appear overwhelming to us. The maturity of our practice is determined by our ability to overcome those obstacles. We need to diagnose, evaluate, and confirm where we stand in our practice, and undertake any tasks for progression to the next stage.

The stages of spiritual practice have already been set out by all the major religions of the world, according to their own standards and perspectives.

In Eastern cultures, a person's character typically proceeds through the ranks of the gifted, the noble, the great, and the wise. Once a person finally reaches the stage of sage, they are greatly esteemed by society. Here are the stages of practice for the traditional Eastern religions of Confucianism and Buddhism.

Confucianism:

The spiritual capacity of knowledge through difficult effort
The spiritual capacity of knowledge from learning
The spiritual capacity of innate knowledge

As well as:
The spiritual capacity for action where we reach the stage of practice through effort and striving
The spiritual capacity for action where we reach the stage of practicing comfortably
The spiritual capacity for action where we enjoy practicing while reaching each stage of practice

Buddhism:

Stream-entrant: Untainted by the six sense objects
Once-to-be-reborn: Free from the constraints of the triple world
Non-returner: Without desire internally and without the sensory conditions of desire externally
Arhat: Having cleaned away all defilements
Bodhisattva: Following the buddha above and delivering sentient beings below
Buddha: Possessing the wisdom and virtues with a myriad of abilities

In addition to the Confucian and Buddhist stages outlined above,

Won-Buddhism defines two sets that more accurately reflect the functioning of the mind. One set details the "four stages of the mind"; the other set outlines the dharma stages.

The Four Stages of Mind

The four-stage model of mind practice consists of Grasping the Mind, Watching the Mind, Forgetting the Mind, and Utilizing the Mind.

Grasping the Mind

To grasp the mind is to bind it to a certain place. Just as we place a yoke on an ox or tie a horse to a post, so too do we direct the mind's attention to a particular point to prevent it from straying elsewhere.

Watching the Mind

Here, we watch the actions of the mind closely, never letting it out of our sight.

Forgetting the Mind

With this, we shed all thoughts as they arise, holding only the mind that is like the void.

Utilizing the Mind

Having grasped the mind, watched the mind and forgetting the mind, we gain the ability to think and act appropriately in all situations.

These represent the four stages of mind capability as a vertical structure with "upper" and "lower" distinctions. They can also be viewed in a horizontal or side by side structure, because circumstances often call for us to demonstrate all four capabilities at the same time.

For example, we may need to focus on grasping the mind, while also demonstrating the watched, absent, and able minds. At other times, watching the mind may be our focus, which we accompany with the seized, absent, and able minds. Still at other times, forgetting the mind is the principal focus, combined with the seized, watched, and able minds. There are also times when utilizing the mind is the central aim that must be joined with the seized, watched, and absent minds. All of these scenarios share the character of a horizontal orientation.

The four stages of the mind were first described in a dharma instruction by Master Chongsan, the Second Head Dharma Master of Won-Buddhism. They offer a remarkable method that no practitioner who seeks to cultivate his mind can afford to ignore. We must discipline ourselves with these four stages on a daily basis, while making sure not to focus solely on any one of them.

Six Stages of Dharma
: The Three Grades and Three Statuses

What are the Three Grades and Three Statuses?

The three grades are the Ordinary grade, the grade of Special Faith, and the grade of the Battle between Dharma and Mara.

The three statuses are the status of *Dharma strong and Mara defeated*, the status of *Beyond the Household*, and the status of *Enlightened Buddha*.

The *Ordinary Grade* is the stage of the beginner's mind, when a person has first discovered and become curious about the existence of a path to practice.

The grade of *Special Faith* is the stage of aspiration, where a person is drawn to explore through curiosity and discovers the path, becoming more certain and sure-footed about it.

The grade of the *Battle Between Dharma and Mara* is the stage of struggle, where, through deep practice of the dharma, it becomes clear what is the dharma and what is Mara, with a fierce confrontation ensuing between the two.

The status of *Dharma Strong and Mara defeated* is the stage of submission, when the ongoing seesaw battle finally ends with a victory for the dharma.

The status of *Beyond the Household* is the stage where practitioners leave behind all mental constraints and embody loving-kindness, considering the whole world as their single household and the four forms of birth as a single family.

The status of *Enlightened Buddha* is the stage of complete freedom, where we are perfectly endowed with buddha's wisdom and virtues. Practitioners of this status possess a great capacity to deliver all living beings.

The first three grades are sentient being worlds, while the latter three statuses are those of sagehood.

These grades and statuses are benchmarks marking the stages of progress of the practitioner. They are a ladder for the practitioner to climb to reach the Buddha land, and they are a guidebook for the long journey of practice.

The Six Stages of Practice
with the Il-Won-Sang Transmission Verse

Transmission Verse

Being into Nonbeing, Nonbeing into Being
Turning and Turning—in the Ultimate,
Being and Nonbeing are Both Empty
Yet This Emptiness is Also Complete

First Stage: Being into Nonbeing

From the place where reality exists (all good dharmas),
We work hard, possessing and developing,
But we release all misleading ideas as well, returning to and resting in a place of nothing.

Second Stage: Nonbeing into Being

In that place devoid of anything, we live comfortably in unbound transcendence,
Until we follow that state to a place of being,
Shaping and sharing a vision that is free and unfettered.

Third Stage: Turning and Turning

When we do not stop at any one place,

When we continue to turn, so that there is no end.

Fourth Stage: In the Ultimate
Our practice deepens and deepens, until finally
We arrive at the ultimate realm, the unequaled realm.

Fifth Stage: Being and Nonbeing are Both Empty
Though we may have arrived,
There is no being in being, nor nonbeing in nonbeing;
Not a trace remains.

Sixth Stage: Yet This Emptiness is Also Complete
We reach the stage that is utterly empty,

Yet perfect and complete with the light of the void and calm, numinous awareness,

With great capacity, infinite wisdom and infinite virtue of the Buddha.

The Pinnacle of Practice

So far the principles of the mind, the principles of practice, and the reality of practice have all been reviewed. All of these represent our journey toward the pinnacle of practice. When we actually arrive at the pinnacle, there is no thought of having arrived or of having comprehended. There is, in fact, nothing. This realm connects with the truth of the universe, it becomes one with it—undivided.

This is also the realm of the non-material, the non-concept, and the non-value. We cannot speak of it as "existing" or "non-existing" nor call it one thing or the other. We cannot say this realm is right or wrong. It is a realm that transcends being and nonbeing, ourselves and others. There must be true emptiness for it to be true nature. Any existence, any definition, any lack of definition, any question of right or wrong is untrue nature. When we abandon all conceptions of right and wrong, that is true nature. We may seek out extraordinary methods to grasp true nature, but how can we call it true nature when we are bound to it by extraordinary methods?

When we arrive at this pinnacle stage, there are phenomena that occurs outside of our awareness: Penetration of the Way, Penetration of Dharma, and Numinous Penetration. *Penetration of the Way* refers to mastery of the great and small, being and nonbeing of heavenly creation, and the right and wrong, and gain and loss of human beings. *Penetration of Dharma* means mastery with enough capability to state the right and wrong and gain and loss of human beings after witnessing the great and small, being and nonbeing of heavenly creation. This creates a dharma that ten thousand generations of sentient beings can adopt as a paragon for emulation. *Numinous Penetration* refers to the stage when our numinous nature becomes clear. We understand the transformations of all things in heaven and earth and the retribution and response of cause and effect for the past, present, and future of human beings: Recognizing them in all their truth without seeing, hearing, or thinking.

Among the dharma instructions of the Buddha, we also find one called the "three knowledges and the six superpowers." The Three Knowledges are: Recollection of Past Lives, the Divine Eye, and the Complete Liberation from Suffering. The Six Superpowers are those of the Divine Eye, the Divine Ear, Knowing the Thoughts of Others, Recollection of Past Lives, Magical Powers, and the Power of the Complete Liberation from Suffering.

The Knowledge of Recollection of Past Lives: The opening of wisdom in viewing our previous lives.

The Knowledge of the Divine Eye: The opening of wisdom to see into the world of truth.

The Knowledge of the Extinction of the Outflows: The brightening of all things that we encounter, leaving no corner of them in darkness.

The Power of the Divine Eye: Mastery of the wisdom to see into things without looking.

The Power of the Divine Ear: Mastery of the wisdom to hear into things without listening.

The Power of Knowing the Thoughts of Others: Entering the minds of others and clearly knowing and understanding what we find there.

The Power of Recollection of Past Lives: Mastering and knowing the fateful existences of previous lives.

Magical Powers: The ability to immediately rush to where one is needed without moving even a step.

The Power of the Extinction of the Outflows: The realm of mastery of the wisdom to fully understand all that we encounter.

All of these may seem fantastic, but they are all phenomena that appear incrementally as we proceed along the path of practice. When we arrive at the end, they open wide to us. It is a matter of truth, neither mystery nor miracle. Although the expressions are somewhat figurative, what is expressed here is true nature.

If the practitioner merely seeks mysticism without any exertion on real work to accumulate merit, then the Three Knowledges and Six Superpowers are truly illusory. Not only would such practitioners fail to deeply and sincerely benefit from their practice they would also comprehend nothing of true value in the end. In fact, such behavior may result in a trap full of defilements, idle thoughts, and desires. Practitioners must therefore be wary.

Once we ascend to the pinnacle of practice, there comes a stage where nothing is beyond our knowledge or our ability. While this is an unerring fact, it is ultimately a matter of the use of our mind, Therefore, it is wise to take heed when inquiring into these stages, so as not to introduce misapprehensions and confusion into our practice.

The ultimate stage of Spiritual Cultivation is Great Liberation; the ultimate stage of Cultivation of Wisdom is Great Enlightenment; and the ultimate stage of Choice in Action is the Great Middle Path.

At every time and every place, our command of the true nature in our daily life must be manifested through *Liberation*, *Great Enlightenment*, and *the Middle Path*. We can tell if one is greatly enlightened or not, through a brief question and answer exchange of a koan.

Although superiors, inferiors, and equals may suggest that someone has seen the true nature and they may pride themselves on having done so, it is impossible to acknowledge "seeing the true nature" unless it emerges in their command of the nature.

When the true nature organically comes forth to practitioners it can be seen in their actions and behavior. This proof of realization happens without the need for a word ever being spoken.

Practitioners may command the skill to speak profusely on matters of theory or universal principles, but if they go no farther than pronouncing their command of The Nature and are mired by delusion, they cannot be said to have mastered enlightenment. "Seeing the nature," will be an empty shell, unless cultivation of the spirit and command of our true nature follows.

The practitioner should also be wary of various traps that may bewilder them in the deeper stages of practice. For example, visions or exaggerated beliefs about the amazing miracles and mysterious superpowers that will emerge. One needs to be aware that while there are similar elements of these in the process of practice, it is not the true nature of practice. Consider this: Jesus was forced to bear the crucifixion despite the powers he possessed; the Buddha was forced to watch the collapse of his father's kingdom, despite the Buddha's own powers; and Confucius had to endure the shame of Daozhi, the legendary big thief. We find some people confounding human minds by boasting of powers to bestow auspicious names, miraculous or occult abilities, or the capability of telling fortunes. We must not let ourselves be taken in by deception. If we do, we may allow ourselves to be taken advantage of. If we avoid being taken in, and proceed with the right dharma and right way of practice by exerting ourselves and accumulating merits, we will be able to reach the pinnacle of practice described above.

It is the Way of flying in the empty space,
Racing on the ground,
Swimming in the water,
And strolling leisurely about.

It is the Way of eating when we are hungry,
Watering our thirsty throat,
Sleeping when we are tired,
And strolling leisurely about.
Is this not the world of the buddha, the world of the Way?

Buddhahood is said to be the final stage at the pinnacle of practice.

Sotaesan, the Founding Master of Won-Buddhism, said, "The great loving-kindness and great compassion of the Buddha radiates more warmth and brightness than the sun. Thus, where this loving-kindness and compassion reach, the ignorant minds of sentient beings melt away into the mind of wisdom; the minds of cruelty melt away into the mind of loving-kindness and compassion; the mind of miserliness and greed melts away into the mind of generosity; and the discriminating mind melts away into the all-encompassing mind. Therefore, the awesome power and radiant brightness of this loving-kindness and compassion are incomparable."

He continued, saying, "The Buddha's unsurpassed, great path is immensely high, deep, and vast; hence, his wisdom and capacity cannot be expressed and recorded either verbally or in writing. However, if I were to give the gist of his teaching, we know only that all sentient beings are subject to birth and death in this lifetime but they do not know of their many other lives; while the Buddha knew the principle that is free from birth and death and the existence of endless lifetimes through the process of rebirth. We do not even understand the fundamental principle governing our own selves, but the Buddha understood the fundamental principle governing all things in the universe. We let ourselves proceed into unwholesome destinies because we cannot always make clear distinctions between choices in life that are wholesome and unwholesome, but the Buddha, after delivering himself, gained the ability to deliver all sentient beings throughout the worlds of the ten directions from unwholesome destinies to wholesome destinies. We do not understand even the suffering and happiness we create for ourselves, but the Buddha understood the suffering and happiness that inadvertently occur as well as those which sentient beings create for themselves. We enjoy the fruits of our merit but can do nothing when it is exhausted, but the Buddha has the ability to restore merit once it is exhausted. We live without discerning whether our wisdom is becoming dull or bright, but the Buddha has the ability to illuminate wisdom that has been dulled and to sustain wisdom once it is attained. We often commit wrongful actions under the influence of our own greed, hatred, and delusion, but the Buddha never acts on greed, hatred, and delusion. We are attached to the existence of all things in the universe but are ignorant of the realm where all things in the universe are nonexistent, but the Buddha knew even the nonexistence amid existence and the existence amid nonexistence. We have no knowledge of either the six destinies of heavenly beings: human beings, asuras, animals, hungry ghosts, and the denizens of hell or the four types of birth: viviparous, oviparous, moisture-born, and metamorphic, but the Buddha knew even the principle governing rebirth between the six destinies and the four types of birth. We take advantage of others for our own benefit, but the Buddha, in dealing with any matter, sought to benefit both oneself and others and, when that became impossible, he found merit and happiness in benefiting others regardless of gain or loss, even at the risk of his own life. We only possess the limited objects that actually belong to us. Our home is only the actual house in which we live, and our family only the people to whom we are related. But the Buddha has called all things in the universe his possessions, the worlds in the ten directions his home, and all sentient beings his family. Hence, our aim is to strive to attain the Buddha's wisdom and abilities and exert ourselves to deliver all sentient beings."

Master Sotesan also said, "Buddhas and bodhisattvas have a Way for being free from hindrances and for remaining autonomous regardless of whether they are walking, standing, sitting, reclining, speaking, keeping silent, active, or at rest. Accordingly, they readily know when to be at rest and when to be active; when to become large and when to be small; when to be bright and when to be dark; and when to live and when to die. In this way, no matter what they do or where they are, they do not deviate even slightly from the rules of the dharma."

And all that remains
Is great loving-kindness and compassion
That only lives and dies and works
For all sentient beings.
We cannot fail to deliver sentient beings once we awaken to the truth
And we cannot fail to awaken to the truth as we deliver sentient beings.
But what exactly is the process by which this highest stage opens up?

The opening of this pinnacle cannot be the same for any two people. Though they may all have completed the same practice under the same teacher, there will be 60 ranks in the resulting capabilities for each of 60 students. All of them will have different innate talents and education and all of them will have dedicated different levels of effort and one pointed mind to their studies.

The same is true for practice.

In practice, too, we can rise gloriously like the sun in the east or rise behind dark clouds, so that one cannot tell exactly when it has happened. We may also see the spectacle of the practitioner rising while shrouded in a gentle mist. Every way is different, depending on the circumstances of the expanse into which the sun rises.

The same is also true for the rising of the sun of wisdom in the mind's void when the mind is completely clear and empty. We may see either sudden enlightenment/sudden cultivation, where the opening is dazzling to the eye or a more gradual opening where we cannot tell when it is happening, as well as other kinds of openings. However, what is important is that the mind opens. No matter how long the process may take, all discriminations of spiritual capacity disappear once we arrive at the ultimate stage. Just as the light illuminates the heavens and earth when all the clouds lift in the sky, the sun shines through no matter how the sky opens.

Having said this, it is crucial to understand that this opening requires both spiritual cultivation and a command of the nature.

A Final Word

We have reached the conclusion of this dharma work, which began with the hope of providing truly critical information about mind training, as well as hopefully preventing future students from wandering aimlessly on their path of practice. While this book is only an introduction, it is designed to give the astute reader an overall sense of the essential elements of mind training and common pitfalls. I hope it will serve as a reliable resource for those who have embarked with sincere determination to engage in their practice.

When we inscribe the true meaning of practice in our mind, we will understand that practice is not something only special people can do. It is something that everyone can and should do. If we practice sincerely and diligently, it will bring great benefit to us and to the world.

Again, it must be understood that practice is not simply the accumulation of knowledge, nor is it a game of ideas. We will not make a single step of progress, if we simply rely on our intelligence or having a clever way with words. We must dedicate ourselves with true effort, stepping forward to do it ourselves. Practice is not something someone else can do for us.

As soon as we attain a sense of the principle of the mind, we should begin our mind practice. To be completely clear, it is not something that interferes with what we are doing now. Rather it can literally be applied directly to what we do, here and now in every moment.

Our best time to begin mind practice is the moment we discover the need for mind practice. Any delay causes us harm and failure to guarantee our progress towards growth on the road ahead.

With this book, may a ray of light shine on all of our paths of mind practice.

About The Author

Venerable Chwasan served as the Fourth Head Dharma Master of Won-Buddhism, succeeding His Holiness Daesan.

He has been a lifelong truth seeker, and has used the wisdom he had attained through spiritual practice as a basis for providing practical solutions for a wide range of areas, from social issues to everyday mindful living.

He entered the Won Buddhist faith at the age of twenty and served as the head minister of the Chongno Won Buddhist Temple in Seoul. He also served on the Supreme Council before being inaugurated as the Fourth Head Dharma Master in 1994.

Since stepping down as the Head Dharma Master in 2006, he has devoted himself to the realization of three great vows: world peace, the reunification of South and North Korea, and healing the mind and heart of the modern individual.

He has written many books, including *The Principles for Training of the Mind*, *Commentary on the Dharma of Timeless Zen*, *The Method of Sitting Meditation*, *We Live as We Believe*, and *To Make a Happy Home*.

Venerable Chwasan envisions a worldwide community of truth and oneness.